POSTAL MONOPOLY

Evaluative Studies

This series of studies seeks to bring about greater understanding and promote continuing review of the activities and functions of the federal government. Each study focuses on a specific program, evaluating its cost and efficiency, the extent to which it achieves its objectives, and the major alternative means—public and private—for reaching those objectives. Yale Brozen, professor of economics at the University of Chicago and an adjunct scholar of the American Enterprise Institute for Public Policy Research, is the director of the program.

POSTAL MONOPOLY

An assessment of the Private Express Statutes

John Haldi
in association with Joseph F. Johnston, Jr.

89572

American Enterprise Institute for Public Policy Research
Washington, D. C.

WITHDRAWN

John Haldi is president of Haldi Associates, Inc., an economic consulting firm located in New York City.

Joseph F. Johnston, Jr., is a partner in the firm of Tufo, Johnston and Allegaert of New York City and a member of the New York Bar.

Evaluative Studies 13, February 1974

ISBN 0-8447-3123-4

Library of Congress Catalog Card No. L.C. 73-93989

© 1974 by American Enterprise Institute for Public Policy Research, Washington, D. C. Permission to quote from or to reproduce materials in this publication is granted when due acknowledgment is made.

Printed in the United States of America

Cover maze reproduced with permission from *Maze Craze*
© 1971 Troubadour Press, San Francisco

HE 6375
. H34

CONTENTS

INTRODUCTION

It is doubtful whether most Americans know that Congress has given the U.S. Post Office Department and its successor, the U.S. Postal Service, an almost complete monopoly over all *letter* mail.[1] Not knowing this, enterprising individuals seek from time to time to earn extra money by delivering, say, Christmas cards or valentines. But as soon as such delivery comes to the attention of the Post Office, the would-be entrepreneur is made aware of a set of federal laws collectively known as the Private Express Statutes.[2] In short order he is forced to cease and desist from his mail-carrying activities.

The basic intent of the Private Express Statutes is to keep anyone except the Post Office from carrying "letters" for a fee over post routes. The initial Private Express law was passed in 1792, but it contained numerous loopholes which invited competition. As technological developments made the language of the 1792 law obsolete (the original definition of post routes obviously did not include railroads or air routes), the law was gradually amended so as to provide an increasingly effective monopoly for the Post Office. By now all loopholes appear to be closed: post routes are defined to include streets, roads, highways, sidewalks, footpaths, railroads, rivers, streams, creeks, air lanes and any other conceivable route over which mail might be physically transported. It is safe to say that today the Post Office has a secure statutory monopoly over virtually all letter mail.

The Private Express Statutes and the postal monopoly are far broader than a literal interpretation of the key word "letter" would suggest. Interpreting what constitutes a letter has been left to the Post Office and the courts, and in making its interpretations, the Post Office has behaved like any profit-maximizing monopolist. So

1

as to maximize the amount of mail subject to the postal monopoly and thus to protect Post Office revenues, it has construed "letter" to be as all-inclusive as possible.[3] Apparently other public policy considerations—service, convenience, speed of delivery, needs of business and commerce—have been heavily discounted by the Post Office in interpreting and enforcing its monopoly.

The purpose of this study is to assess the impact of the Private Express Statutes and to consider whether the Postal Service should continue to enjoy a statutory monopoly over letter mail. The fact that a government-enforced monopoly has been endured for so long is not sufficient justification for its continuation. Like any other monopoly, the postal monopoly should commend itself unequivocally to the public good, or else it should be abolished.

Since 1971, when the Post Office Department was transformed into a government corporation, the quality of mail service has deteriorated alarmingly. Apparently because of the growth in mail volume, there is need for additional capacity and expedited services which the Postal Service is failing to provide. This is an appropriate time, therefore, to subject the Private Express Statutes and the postal monopoly to critical review. It is time to discover whether the postal monopoly is necessary and economical, or whether it has outlived any usefulness it may have had and is now a barrier to further progress.

Chapter I of this study, for which Joseph Johnston, Jr., is largely responsible, reviews the legal history of the Private Express Statutes, while Chapter II reviews the history of competition in the carriage of letters. Chapter III discusses the nature of possible future competition, with special emphasis on the influence which the Private Express Statutes are likely to have. Chapter IV contains a discussion of policy issues.

In the conclusion—to anticipate—it is pointed out that the statutory postal monopoly has no economic justification. The monopoly is no longer an important source of governmental revenue and in no way promotes better or cheaper mail service. In fact, it probably impedes the development of better systems for delivering written communications.

CHAPTER I

LEGAL HISTORY

Government-provided mail service dates at least from classical times when kings and war-leaders needed a means of communicating with their armies in the field. Because of the military importance of written communication, it was inevitable that mail service would be provided primarily by monarchs and generals. Throughout the world government domination of the transportation of mail has been the rule down to the present time.

In the United States the government has had a monopoly over transportation of letters for more than 175 years. The Constitution itself merely empowers Congress "to establish Post Offices and post Roads." However, since 1792, specific legislation has reserved to the federal government the exclusive right to carry letters. What constitutes a "letter" in the eyes of the law and the Post Office is a complicated question. Today a combination of legislation, regulations, court rulings, and decisions and opinions of the solicitor of the Post Office Department decides whether an item must be transmitted through the mail or whether it can legally be transmitted in other ways.

This chapter traces the history of the postal monopoly and of legislation passed to preserve the monopoly, outlines the conditions under which letters are exempted from the Private Express Statutes, notes the emergence of the United States Postal Service, and discusses its 1973 proposals to amend the postal regulations.

This chapter was contributed by Joseph F. Johnston, Jr. Its first three sections appeared in substantially the same form in Joseph F. Johnston, Jr., "United States Postal Monopoly," *The Business Lawyer* (January 1968), and are included here with the permission of the American Bar Association and its Section of Corporation, Banking and Business Law.

History of the Postal Monopoly to Recent Times

The intricacies of the U.S. postal monopoly can be better understood after a brief look at the history of governmental postal services. Those postal services that existed in the ancient world were used primarily by rulers for the prompt conveyance of military orders and were only occasionally made available to favored private citizens.[1] Government monopoly of the posts was an accepted practice of the national monarchies during the European Renaissance. On the continent, Emperors Maximilian and Charles V granted the concession for the carriage of letters to the Counts of Thurn and Taxis.[2]

Tudor and Stuart England. In sixteenth century England, the monopoly was retained by the monarchs themselves, largely because they feared that private letter carriers would be used to carry out treasonable plots. Letter writing among private citizens was carefully supervised.[3] It may be noted that the postal monopoly in England was originally designed for political purposes rather than to produce revenue for the crown.

In the seventeenth century, however, the British public began to make extensive use of the postal service, and the monopoly became quite profitable. During this period the practice arose of "farming out" the postal patent, and the revenues arising from it, to favorites of the king. Attempts by merchants to provide their own postal services along with their trading activities were suppressed.[4] The Cromwellian government also resisted attempts by independent carriers to provide mail service. An act of Parliament in 1657 reasserted the postal monopoly, although it contained two exceptions: letters relating to goods carried could be transported by carriers along with the goods, and persons were permitted to send letters by messengers "on purpose for their own affairs."[5] These two exemptions from the postal monopoly have survived the vicissitudes of three centuries. They remain, with verbal modifications, in the American law today.

The postal monopoly was continued after the Restoration, but the king's subjects perversely continued to employ illegal means to transport letters. The reason seems to have been that the official service simply was not adequate to meet the growing demand. Carriers of merchandise handled letters that did not relate to their cargo, and stagecoach drivers and passengers began to carry letters for others.[6] These two means of evading the law were so widely used both in England and in America that they could almost be described as traditional.

4

In 1680, the famous London "penny post" was established by one Dockwra who argued, with considerable justice, that his service did not conflict with the government monopoly because the government provided no comparable service. The government's response was to harass Dockwra with legal action, and finally to take over his service altogether and make it part of the official monopoly. Nevertheless, the pressures leading to evasions continued to be irresistible. In 1709, Charles Povey used bell ringers to collect letters, which he delivered anywhere in London for a halfpenny. The Post Office prosecuted Povey, who was convicted and fined, and then it adopted his system for the government service. In 1711 an act was passed reorganizing the entire postal system. Carriers were forbidden to transport letters that did not concern their goods, and stagecoaches were forbidden to carry mail. Letters carried on board ships were required to be turned over to the nearest post office by the captain immediately upon landing (indicating another popular method of evasion). In spite of the statute, evasion of the postal monopoly continued to be widespread in eighteenth century Britain.[7]

Colonial America. In America, meanwhile, the postal system developed as an offshoot of the British monopoly. In 1692, William and Mary granted a patent to Thomas Neale giving him a monopoly of the colonial posts, including all profits.[8] A number of the colonial legislatures passed laws confirming the Neale patent within their respective jurisdictions, but some of them carved out broad exceptions.[9] The New York statute, for instance, exempted all letters going up and down the Hudson or to and from Long Island—which constituted most of the correspondence in the colony during that period.[10] These exemptions were symptomatic of a continuing undercurrent of colonial hostility toward the British postal monopoly throughout the prerevolutionary period. In 1718 the Virginia House of Burgesses declared that the colonists could not be taxed without their consent and exempted all merchants' letters from the payment of postage. This position enraged Governor Spotswood, who termed the colonists' argument "as ridiculous . . . as arrogant." [11] As noted above, the statute of 1711 had explicitly forbidden all private transportation of letters except those relating to cargo. Nevertheless, in the colonies there was constant evasion of the law. It was reported that many stage drivers gave letters to the passengers to carry, or tied the letters to bundles of straw so that it could be claimed they were related to cargo.[12]

In 1775, the various colonies set up their own postal systems, which became known as the "constitutional post." This gained swift acceptance, bringing about the demise of the official British system.

The Continental Congress established a postal system in July 1775 and appointed Benjamin Franklin postmaster general. Nevertheless, it appears that private posts continued to be established during the Revolution.[13]

The Articles of Confederation gave Congress "the sole and exclusive right and power of . . . establishing and regulating post offices from one State to another, throughout all the United States, and exacting such postage on the papers passing through the same as may be requisite to defray the expenses of the said office . . ." (Article 9, paragraph 4). Three points are of interest here: first, the words "sole and exclusive" clearly are evidence of intent to establish a monopoly; second, the monopoly was to apply only to interstate service; and third, postage was only to be sufficient to cover expenses, indicating that the new government could not "tax" its citizens in the form of postal fees, as the British had done, in order to raise revenues for general purposes. In 1782 the Continental Congress passed a revised postal law providing for a monopoly but allowing an exception in the case of specially engaged messengers. However, there continued to be a large volume of letters carried illegally. Apparently, during the period of the confederation the Post Office was unable to enforce its monopoly.[14]

The federal Constitution, adopted in 1789, provides that Congress shall have power "to establish Post Offices and post Roads" (Article 1, section 8). Significantly, the words "sole and exclusive," which appeared in the Articles of Confederation, were eliminated. This omission raises the question whether it was intended that Congress under the new charter was to have a monopoly. More precisely, the constitutional question is whether a postal monopoly is "necesary and proper" for carrying out the power to establish post offices and post roads. An appealing argument can be made that it is hardly necessary to forbid private citizens and businesses to carry letters in order to be able to construct postal facilities. The few courts which have considered the question, however, have acquiesced in the constitutionality of the monopoly—although without much analysis of the question.[15]

The best reason for holding the monopoly constitutional lies in the history of the British and colonial postal systems, in which the governmental monopoly had been an integral, though not always a successful, feature. There seems to be no evidence one way or the other in the debates at the Constitutional Convention or in other sources of the period.[16] *Federalist* Number 42 states that "the power of establishing post roads must, in every view, be a harmless power and may, perhaps, by judicious management become productive of great public conveniency." The fact was that private enterprise, in its infancy in the late eighteenth century, could not have attempted to supply the postal requirements of a frontier nation. Since it was taken for granted that only the central government could provide this service, the question of government monopoly was never seriously considered.

Thus the issue of the constitutionality of the postal monopoly must, in default of other evidence, be answered by history. The framers must have had in mind the fact that for 150 years, both in Britain and in the colonies, the postal service had been a monopoly of the government and that it had remained a monopoly under the Articles of Confederation. The first act of the new Congress with respect to the postal establishment confirms this conjecture. The act of September 22, 1789, provided that "the regulations of the post-office shall be the same as they last were under the resolutions and ordinances of the late Congress."[17] And the "late Congress," as noted above, clearly established a postal monopoly. It is hardly likely that the first Congress could have misconstrued the intent of the Founding Fathers on this point. The constitutionality of the monopoly may accordingly be accepted. On the other hand, it seems equally clear that the Constitution does not require a government monopoly of the transportation of mail. The practical problem, therefore, is to determine the extent of the monopoly granted by enactments of Congress and the desirability of continuing the monopoly.

From the Constitution to 1845. Following the temporary postal act of 1789, which simply carried forward the laws of the confederation, Congress in 1792 passed the first comprehensive postal statute under the new Constitution. Section 14 of this law prohibited any private person from carrying any letters for hire, or from setting up a private post for hire on any post road or by vessel, but in either case only if the revenue of the general post office be injured.[18] The sole express exception was that letters might be sent "by special messenger," an exception that has persisted, with modifications, to the present time. The law also carried forward the prohibitions in British law against ships making entry into port or breaking bulk without delivering all letters to the postmaster.[19] An amendment in 1794 added two additional exceptions—letters directed to the owner of the conveyance and letters directed to the person to whom any package is to be delivered (the latter being the equivalent of the traditional exception for letters relating to cargo).[20] A law of 1810 readopted the private express provisions virtually unchanged, except that it extended the prohibition against private carriage of letters to include not only post roads but "any road adjacent or parallel to an established post road." [21]

The first comprehensive revision of the postal laws was accomplished by the act of March 3, 1825.[22] The monopoly provision of this act was directed toward the vehicle which carried letters illegally rather than toward persons establishing a private post. It provided that no stage or other vehicle which regularly performed trips on a post road or road parallel to it should carry letters, except letters that related to some part of the cargo. The "special messenger" exception was retained. The 1825 statute would not have prevented the establishment of a private post other than by "vehicle" (that is, it would have permitted a foot or horse post). This loophole was narrowed by Congress in 1827 by the enactment of a statute prohibiting private persons from setting up any foot or horse post for the conveyance of letters on any post road.[23]

It soon became apparent, however, that there were abundant opportunities for avoiding the 1825 and 1827 laws. Ambitious entrepreneurs were not slow to seize them. In the 1830s, spurred by high postal rates and slow mail service, a number of private express companies flourished along the eastern seaboard, catering particularly to the needs of businessmen.[24] These enterprises took advantage of two weaknesses of the legislation of the 1820s which the draftsmen probably could not have foreseen: the unwillingness of the courts to hold the owner of a vehicle responsible for letters carried by a passenger and the fact that the 1827 statute applied to foot and horse posts but not to railroads. For instance, in United States v. Adams,[25] the court held that the owner of a stage or vessel that carries a passenger who is transporting letters may not be held liable for the statutory penalty.[26] The court conceded that this practice had resulted in a substantial revenue loss to the Post Office Department, but was unwilling to extend the statute beyond its scope on this ground alone. In United States v. Kimball, it was held that the 1827 statute applied only to foot or horse posts and not to the transportation of letters in railroad cars, even though, as the court observed, the injury to the postal service may have been just as great.[27]

The Post Office was of course alarmed at the growth of the private express companies. The report of the postmaster general for 1843 attributed a decline in revenues to "the operations of the numerous private posts, under the name of expresses, which have sprung into existence within the past few years, extending themselves over the mail routes between the principal cities and towns.... That these private posts are engaged in the business of transporting letters and mail matter for pay ... is a fact which will not be seriously controverted."[28] Referring to the *Adams* case, the postmaster general urged Congress to pass new legislation to correct the defect in the existing statutes. He conceded that many persons believed the governmental monopoly was "odious" and "ought to be abolished" and noted that this viewpoint was "urged by a portion of a powerful press, and sustained by the influence of those whose interests are involved." He concluded by summarizing the economic argument which has been used throughout modern American (and British) history to support the postal monopoly against private competition. "These private expresses will only be found to operate upon the great and profitable thoroughfares between great commercial points, whilst the extremes are left to depend upon the operations of the United States mail, crippled and broken down for the want of means."[29]

From 1845 to Recent Times. Congress in 1845 attempted to remedy the defects in the law which had apparently led to the unfortunate situation described in the postmaster general's reports. The law of March 3, 1845, substantially strengthened the restrictions against "private expresses," as they were now officially called for the first time.[30] In place of the 1827 prohibition against foot or horse posts, the new law forbade "any private express" for the conveyance of letters by regular trips, or at stated periods or intervals, from one city or town to any other city or town between which the United States mail was regularly transported. The method of conveyance became irrelevant. The penalty for violating the law was also increased.

Another section of the law provided penalties for owners of vehicles who knowingly transported persons employed as a private express for the conveyance of letters. This was obviously designed to stop the practice held lawful in the *Adams* and *Pomeroy* cases. In addition, the statute was broadened to reach the *sender* of the letter, who had previously been reachable only through a vague "aiding and abetting" section that had not produced any convictions. The 1845 law retained the exemption for letters relating to cargo or articles, and it added a provision (which still remains in the law) permitting the conveyance of letters by private hands without compensation. However, it narrowed the "special messenger" exemption by restricting it to special messengers "employed only for the single particular occasion." (This change has also remained in the law.) Another exception added a few years later, permitted prestamped envelopes, properly sealed and addressed, to be sent outside the mail.[31] This exception has also persisted to the present time. It does no harm from the Post Office point of view, of course, because the postal revenues are fully protected by the requirement of prior stamping.

The 1845 legislation essentially placed the Private Express Statutes in the form in which they remain today. Neither the 1845 law, however, nor the few changes in it succeeded in eliminating what the Post Office Department regarded as the illicit carriage of mail. For instance, the report of the postmaster general for 1845 stated that in spite of the passage of the new act "plunderers of the public revenues" continued to carry letters outside of the mails.[32] A widely circulated pamphlet by Joshua Leavitt, published in 1848 and entitled *Cheap Postage,* emphasized that the 1845 legislation had failed to achieve its purpose of eliminating private expresses. Leavitt cited the existence of over 200 private expresses (most of which carried letters) in the Boston area alone.[33] The cure, according to Leavitt, was cheaper postage and better service. "The post-office must be enabled *to recommend itself to the public mind.* It must secure to itself a virtual monopoly, by the greater security, expedition, punctuality, and cheapness, with which it does its work, than can be reached by any private enterprise."[34] He subscribed to the opinion of Rowland Hill, the British postal reformer, that with the resources of the government behind it, the Post Office Department ought to be able to defeat competition without resorting to penal statutes. The evidence, in short, indicates that evasion (or at least "avoidance") of the postal monopoly continued into the 1850s, caused in part by the inefficiency and tardiness of mail delivery during this period.[35]

Few changes have been made in the Private Express Statutes during the past century and a quarter. In 1872 the statutes were recodified.[36] In 1879 another exception was grafted onto the law: it was declared lawful to receive and deliver mail, properly stamped, at the nearest post office. In 1909 the statutes were once more recodified. At this time, an exception was added for such letters "as relate . . . to the current business of the carrier."[37] The "current business" exemption wrote into the statute what the attorney general had said in 1896 was already there.[38]

A law of June 22, 1934,[39] restricted the "special messenger" exemption by adding the requirement that no more than twenty-five letters be carried. In 1948, the Private Express Statutes were recodified without substantial change as part of Title 18 of the United States Code.[40]

Shoring Up the Postal Monopoly

In a free enterprise system competition tends to arise wherever entrepreneurs see a way to earn a profit. This is especially true when a field of endeavor does not have high costs of entry. Throughout history the sorting and delivering of mail has required an insignificant amount of capital equipment. Time after time competition has arisen whenever the Post Office has not been alert to the changing needs of the public or the changing means of delivering mail. Enterprising schemes have temporarily cracked the postal monopoly and forced the Post Office to ask Congress to close "loopholes" in the Private Express Statutes.

In response, the Post Office Department has used the Private Express Statutes to protect its revenues, despite the ill effects which this protection might have on either the individuals attempting to improve the mail service or the members of the public using or benefiting from the private service. The behavior of the Post Office has not differed from what one would expect from any monopoly. To protect postal revenues, Congress has from time to time placed restrictions on (1) the routes over which mail may be carried and (2) conditions under which any private messenger may carry letters.

Restrictions on "Post Routes." The earliest private express law applied only to "post roads" between specifically designated points.[41] In 1810, the restrictions were extended to include not only post roads but "any road adjacent or parallel to an established post road." [42] The 1845 postal law made the prohibition against carriage of mail by stagecoaches and railroads applicable to any "post route" (a term which, from the context, must have been meant to include any route over which the United States mail was carried),[43] although the general prohibition against private expresses (including foot posts) only applied to conveyance of letters *between* cities.[44] This loophole led to the establishment of foot posts for mail delivery within city limits,[45] which in turn resulted in the passage of legislation applying the restriction against foot and horse posts to all post routes established *in* any city or town.[46]

Since 1872, the general prohibition against private expresses has applied to any post route, wherever established.[47] Under this law, it was held that the conveyance of letters over the streets of New York was unlawful.[48] The Post Office Department has also held that the conveyance of letters by means of pneumatic tubes along or under the streets of a city by private persons would be unlawful.[49] Where an office building is served by United States letter carriers who deliver mail directly to the offices, the department has said that the corridors of the building are post routes and that a private express within the building is therefore unlawful.[50]

If there is no transportation of letters over *any* route, it follows that there is no violation of the statute. Thus, when an enterprising

Boston businessman established a "private post office," where he received letters for a fee and delivered them to the addressees who came into the office to pick them up, the Post Office Department held that there was no violation.[51]

It should be remembered that the Private Express Statutes apply not only to transportation over post routes but also to transportation between towns or other places "between which the mail is regularly carried," [52] whether or not the transportation between such places occurs over a post route.[53]

Requirement of Regularity. There was no requirement of regularity in the prohibition against private expresses by land until the law of March 3, 1825, which provided that no stage or other vehicle which *regularly* performed trips on a post road or a road parallel to it should convey letters.[54] The words "by regular trips or at stated periods" appeared in the 1845 law [55] and have remained ever since. In *United States v. Easson*,[56] it was held that daily deliveries were "regular trips and at stated periods." The court said that "to constitute regularity it is not essential that the minute or hour of the departures of the messenger should be always the same." [57] The court intimated, however, that there might not be sufficient regularity to satisfy the statute if the customers were to summon messengers from a central source, but only when they were required for a particular delivery.

This hint was apparently not lost on a Chicago lawyer who, many years later, devised an ingenious scheme for private mail service within an office building. The customers were insurance agents who had separate offices in the Insurance Exchange Building and who operated a joint clearinghouse in the same building. The clearinghouse hired messengers who were made available in a "pool." Any participating insurance agent could summon a messenger by pushing a button, and the messenger would then deliver the agent's letters to other agents or to the clearinghouse. The Post Office Department held that the plan did not violate the Private Express Statutes.[58] The point of this case seems to be that where messengers are available on call and do not make any trips at predetermined intervals to pick up or deliver mail, there is no regularity and the private express prohibitions are inapplicable.

In 1935, the Post Office Department and the Justice Department proposed legislation to close what they regarded as a loophole by eliminating the regularity requirement.[59] What they objected to was a service offered by telegraph companies and others whereby a business would accumulate a large number of outgoing letters, then call the messenger service and request a messenger. The telegraph companies argued that the service was not regular and that in addi-

12

tion (1) the messengers were agents of the senders, not of the carrier, and (2) the carriage was by special messenger employed for a particular occasion only.[60] Congress took no action on the proposed legislation.

Specific Statutory Exemptions

The prohibitions of the Private Express Statutes apply only to "letters." They do not apply to packages or parcels not containing letters, nor do they apply to newspapers, periodicals, or unaddressed advertising matter. The question of what constitutes a "letter" has been the subject of heated controversy since the adoption of the Private Express Statutes.

Non-letters that Are Letters. Over the years the Post Office has adopted complex and conflicting interpretations of what constitutes a letter. As noted above, the one consistent thread running through these interpretations is that the Post Office has construed the term so as to restrict competition and maximize its own revenues. For example, the term "letter" has been interpreted to include machine-processed records such as punched-hole cards, bills, receipts, price lists, and virtually all other common business documents. The most recent interpretations by the Postal Service will be discussed below in the section on Proposed Amendments to the Postal Regulations.

Letters that Are Not Letters. Documents that fall under certain exemptions may be sent outside the mails regardless of whether they are otherwise classified as letters.

(1) *Letters which "relate to some part of the cargo . . . or to some article carried may be carried"* outside the mails.[61] The "cargo" exemption is one of the oldest of all exemptions to the postal monopoly. Although it appears only in section 1694 and not in section 1696, the cargo exemption has always been interpreted as applicable to the Private Express Statutes as a whole. The regulations in effect before the recent postal reorganization [62] appeared on their face to be more restrictive than the statute, by limiting the exemption to letters which related *exclusively* to cargo or articles carried and by providing that any information extraneous to the shipment takes the letter out of the exemption. The statute merely provides that the letter must relate to *some part* of the cargo or to an article carried. One court, however, has supported the stricter interpretation by stating that it was the intention of Congress "to allow a letter to be sent accompanying any article of property, provided it related merely

to the article of property or money sent, and did not concern any other subject." [63]

(2) *Letters which "relate ... to the current business of the carrier" may be carried outside the mails.*[64] The "current business" exemption, like the cargo exemption, appears only in section 1694, but has always been assumed to be applicable to the other sections of the Private Express Statutes as well. The current business exemption was added to the law in 1909.[65] However, long before that time the Post Office Department had taken the position that the Private Express Statutes applied only to carriage of letters for other persons. The department had generally not objected to any person or firm carrying letters relating to its own business.[66] It should be emphasized that the use of the word "carrier" does not mean that the exemption is restricted to common carriers. Any firm or corporation is permitted to carry letters relating to its own business using its own regular employees.[67]

(3) *Letters properly stamped may be delivered to the nearest post office or mail car.*[68] This provision was adopted by Congress in 1879,[69] possibly as a result of a ruling by the Post Office Department in the preceding year that it was unlawful for a private party to operate a service for placing subscribers' letters on mail trains.[70] The letters must bear the proper postage for transmission through the mails from the point of origin.[71] It is also permissible to establish a service for collecting letters at the post office and delivering them to the addressees, so long as the letters remain unopened. In addition, letters received through the mails at one office of a firm may be forwarded by surface means outside the mails without the payment of additional postage so long as they remain unopened.[72]

(4) *Letters may be carried "by private hands without compensation."* [73] This exemption is traceable to section 11 of the law of March 3, 1845.[74] It has been held that the "no compensation" exemption does not permit a carrier of merchandise to carry a customer's letters (unrelated to the merchandise) even though no separate charge is made for the letters.[75] In such case, the carrier is regarded as compensated for the entire service performed, including the carriage of letters.[76]

(5) *Letters may be carried "by special messenger employed for the particular occasion only" (limited to twenty-five letters).*[77] It is not clear why this exemption is needed in view of the fact that the statute applies only to conveyance of letters "by regular trips or at stated periods." This would seem to exclude a trip by a special

14

messenger for a particular occasion. The reason is probably historical: the "special messenger" exemption was in the original 1792 private express law,[78] which did not contain any requirement of regularity. When the element of regularity was included in the statute in 1825,[79] the special messenger exemption was left in as well. The words "for the particular occasion only" make it clear that the exemption "applies only to isolated instances and not to cases . . . where it is proposed to make . . . deliveries in considerable numbers and upon numerous occasions." [80]

(6) *Letters on which postage is prepaid may be carried outside the mails.*[81] This exemption was introduced into the law in 1852.[82] It permits letters to be carried by private express or other means outside the mails, so long as appropriate postage is paid and the other requirements of Title 39, United States Code, section 901 are followed. This provides a method by which businessmen and others can take advantage of the convenience of private express services without damage to the revenues of the Post Office Department. It also means, of course, that those who take advantage of this exemption are forced to pay twice for one conveyance of mail, and that the Post Office Department is receiving compensation although it performs no service and may not even attempt to offer comparable service.

Emergence of the Postal Service

The Report of the President's Commission on Postal Organization. This report was submitted to the President in June 1968.[83] It concluded that the postal system as organized was not capable of meeting the demands of the nation's growing economy and population, and called for sweeping organizational changes. Specifically, the report recommended that Congress charter a government-owned corporation to operate the postal service—a recommendation that was ultimately carried out.

The report treated the issue of the postal monopoly only peripherally. The commission concluded that "the postal monopoly provided by the Private Express Statutes should be preserved, although not necessarily in its present form," [84] and suggested that the rules be relaxed to permit organizations to use private express for intra-company mail in situations where the Post Office provided inadequate service.[85] The conclusion that the postal monopoly should be retained was based upon two premises, both of which were assumed without argument: first, that the Post Office "has an element of 'natural' monopoly—the waste of having several companies dupli-

15

cating daily deliveries to almost every house is apparent"[86] and, second, that "the postal service is particularly vulnerable to 'cream-skimming' in the high-volume, high-value segments of its market, e.g., delivery within or between downtown districts of major cities."[87]

No satisfactory arguments were set forth to support either of these assumptions. Nor did the report state why it was fair for business users in high-volume segments to subsidize other users of the mails. While the "slight relaxation" of the rules recommended for business users might be useful to them, the commission did not say why this relaxation should be confined to "intra-company" mail rather than offered to all users who were suffering from inadequate service.

Creation of the U.S. Postal Service. In 1970, Congress organized the United States Postal Service as "an independent establishment of the executive branch," to be directed by a board of governors.[88] The legislation became effective on July 1, 1971. The existing statutory provisions establishing the postal monopoly were left intact. Congress did not act upon the commission's advice to permit a "slight relaxation" of the rules, although the section permitting the Postal Service to "suspend the operation" of prohibitions on the carriage of letters outside the mails was retained.[89] Under this provision, the Postal Service subsequently proposed suspending the private express prohibitions for certain types of intra-company and other mail (see below).

Recent Litigation. Because of the continuing inability of the U.S. Postal Service to provide adequate delivery, private postal systems have proliferated. One result has been litigation by unions of postal employees.

One such case involved a private corporation, Independent Postal System of America, Inc., which offered to deliver addressed Christmas cards within certain cities and sold private postage stamps (at five cents per stamp) to users of the service. Prior to 1971, the Independent Postal System had confined its operation to delivery of parcels, newspapers, magazines and unaddressed advertising matter, all of which fell within the various exceptions to the postal monopoly. Shortly before Christmas 1971, a union representing employees of the United States Postal Service brought suit in federal district court in Oklahoma for an injunction to prevent the Independent Postal System from delivering the Christmas cards. The district court held that the plaintiff union had standing to sue and that an injunction against the defendants, Independent Postal System of America, Inc., and its president, should be granted.[90] In finding that the union had

standing to bring the case, the court said that if the defendants' operation was permitted to continue "the approximately two-hundred
thousand members represented by Plaintiff's organization would be
injured in fact by a significant loss of work time, overtime, employment opportunities, future pension and insurance benefits and in
morale." [91] The court concluded that Congress had granted the U.S.
government a monopoly over the carriage of letters, pursuant to civil
and criminal statutes.[92] Finally, the court decided that Christmas
cards were letters within the meaning of the statutes and existing
regulations, even though the cards contained no personal message.[93]
The proposed delivery of Christmas cards was therefore a violation
of the postal monopoly and should be enjoined. The court concluded
by observing that the proposed delivery of Christmas cards would
constitute a "widespread public nuisance."

The defendants appealed to the circuit court which, in affirming
the judgment of the district court,[94] accepted the "cream-skimming"
argument traditionally employed by the Post Office Department in
support of its monopoly:

> The defendants by their proposed operation would
> break this monopoly and siphon off what was described as
> the "cream" of the postal operation, i.e., the delivery of
> certain letters—Christmas cards in various metropolitan
> areas without payment of United States postage—which
> would otherwise be delivered by the letter carriers repre-
> sented by the plaintiff. The obvious effect of the de-
> fendants' proposed operation would be to reduce gross
> postal revenues. And reduced postal revenues would in-
> evitably have adverse effect on the general employment
> statutes [sic] of the plaintiff's members.[95]

In another case involving the same defendants, however, a Michigan
district court held that the union lacked standing to sue.[96] The court
reasoned that enforcement of criminal sanctions should properly be
left to the discretion of the Post Office Department rather than to
private litigants such as labor unions.

Obviously, the conflict between the Oklahoma and Michigan
decisions must ultimately be resolved by the Supreme Court or by
Congress. In the meantime, no matter whether the government en-
forces the postal monopoly, the question of private enforcement (by
unions or others) will remain in doubt.

Proposed Amendments to the Postal Regulations

On June 29, 1973, the Postal Service proposed amendments to the
postal regulations which would redefine the term "letter" and

suspend the Private Express Statutes for certain types of mail.[97] In an introduction to the proposed rule changes, the general counsel of the Postal Service stated that, after a thorough study, "the Postal Service has concluded that changes in the Statutes are unnecessary but that certain administrative practices can and should be improved."[98]

The service proposed that a "letter" be defined simply but comprehensively as "a message in or on a physical object sent to a specific address."[99] The proposed version is more restrictive than prior interpretations. Certain current exceptions to the definition of "letter" are eliminated, among them (a) matter conveying information already known to the addressee, (b) checks and other commercial papers, (c) legal papers and documents, (d) matter sent for auditing and preparation of bills, and (e) matter sent for filing or storage. Thus, checks, notes, bonds, stock certificates, deeds, leases, and other commercial and legal papers would be deemed to be "letters" under the proposed regulations and would accordingly be subject to the Private Express Statutes. The elimination of the exceptions in categories (a), (d) and (e) may have some reasonable justification since these materials are arguably intended to convey information. However, there would seem to be little justification for considering checks, securities, and legal documents as letters. Although the general counsel's introduction states that these documents are "messages, conveying information of several kinds," this interpretation is in fact unreasonable because the basic purpose of these instruments is to evidence legal rights rather than to convey information.

While tightening the definition of "letter," however, the Postal Service proposes to mitigate the impact of the Private Express Statutes by suspending them for four different categories of mail.

(1) "Interoffice communications between offices and branches of the same corporation, partnership, or other organization when transmission must be and is completed within 12 hours or by not later than the opening of the addressee's business on his next working day."[100] This exemption would appear to be of limited use because of its restriction to offices and branches of the same corporation or partnership, leaving deliveries to subsidiaries, affiliates, agencies, and other related offices subject to the prohibitions against private express. This is an arbitrary limitation and disregards the realities of modern business organization. Further, the twelve-hour limitation is impractical when there is no assurance in many areas that the Postal Service can provide twelve-hour or even forty-eight-hour delivery. Finally, there is no apparent reason for discriminating in favor of large corporations which have many branch offices and against businesses, small

and large, which may not have branch offices but may wish to use private express for delivering bills to customers, payments to suppliers, and so on.

(2) "Data processing materials conveyed to or back from a company-owned or independent data processing center, when transmission must be and is completed within 12 hours or by not later than the opening of the addressee's business on his next working day." [101] This provision is obviously tailored to meet the specific needs of businesses with large volumes of computerized data processing. It is not clear why accounting records delivered to an accountant, or business records delivered to a central office other than a "data processing center," should not receive similar treatment. In this case also, the twelve-hour limitation seems arbitrary.

(3) "Checks and other financial instruments, such as stock certificates, promissory notes, bonds and other negotiable securities, when shipped between financial institutions or in bulk to financial institutions." [102] This provision exempts financial documents, but *only* when shipped to or between financial institutions. No reason is given to explain why banks should be exempt with respect to checks, bonds, and other such documents, while corporate issuers of securities and dividend checks, brokerage firms, insurance companies and utilities would not be exempt. All of these organizations transmit large amounts of commercial and financial paper, and it would seem to be in the public interest to permit them all to expedite deliveries by using private express.

(4) Newspapers and periodicals. This exemption is consistent with past history and interpretation, since these publications have not generally been considered as "letters."

It is noteworthy that, under the proposed regulations, persons intending to establish private express services in the areas permitted under paragraphs (1) and (2) would have to notify the Postal Service before beginning operations and file a detailed statement of the scope of the proposed operations. In addition, private express operators would be required to file annual reports giving details of the services provided, including traffic volumes, delivery times, rates, gross revenues, and operating margins. It appears that the Postal Service plans to closely monitor the operating results of private express companies when and if the new exemptions become effective.

The authors understand that the Postal Service intends to issue a new version of its proposed regulations which will include changes made in response to numerous comments.

The proposed suspension of the Private Express Statutes would apply only to those provisions of the statutes contained in Title 39 of the United States Code. It would not apply to the penal provisions contained in Title 18 of the United States Code, sections 1694-1699. Indeed it is doubtful whether the Postal Service has the authority to suspend the operation of the latter sections: congressional action would appear to be necessary. Therefore, assuming the regulations are adopted, the prospective operator of a private express service for interoffice communications or for data processing materials would be in a difficult position. The statutory prohibitions in Title 18 against carriage of "letters" would remain in force, even though the Postal Service has proposed the suspension of certain prohibitions contained in Title 39. The private carrier would face the risk of action by some other agency of the government, or by a private party such as a labor union.

The best solution to this prospective problem of statutory and administrative inconsistency would be for Congress to review the postal monopoly and to determine whether the Private Express Statutes should be preserved at all and, if so, what exemptions should be permitted.

CHAPTER II

HISTORY OF COMPETITION IN THE UNITED STATES

For the last four centuries governments have explicitly reserved to themselves a monopoly over letter mail. Although they have often "farmed out" their postal monopolies for a fee, there is no evidence that any government has ever encouraged private entrepreneurs to offer independent postal services. This stands in sharp contrast to government behavior in other areas of public service—railroads, air transportation, electric service, telephone service, pipelines, or even agriculture or housing. In these areas, the U.S. government has historically encouraged innovation and expansion of the private sector. It is interesting to note that despite unrelenting government efforts to the contrary, both in this country and elsewhere, competition from private posts has persisted and at times even flourished.

At least since the 1600s the basic scenario of postal competition has been the same. First the government's mail service is deficient. Then an enterprising individual decides that he can make a profit by offering faster or cheaper mail service than that provided by the government. Letter writers start using the private service. The government post office senses an impending loss of revenue and may even feel chagrin at being shown to be second-best in service or efficiency. Government then takes action to force the private challengers out of existence. On occasion, postal officials even implicitly honor the creativity of the private entrepreneurs by adopting their methods. Complete suppression of competition rings down the curtain until the next performance.

The scenario highlights the basic policy issue: should the postal monopoly be preserved? This chapter looks at postal competition in the United States for the light that may be shed on this question.

History of Competition before 1940

It is conceivable that throughout history citizens have complained about poor postal service as much as they have about the weather. Certainly poor postal service is nothing new. Mr. Dockwra's innovative penny post was by no means a singular case. Law enforcement was apparently less efficient in those days. Also, postal rates were high enough to earn net revenues for the government, which provided those offering cheaper or better services an opportunity to compete profitably. Evasion of the postal monopoly appears to have been widespread throughout the eighteenth century.

The British postal experience was duplicated in the American colonies, where private posts flourished before and during the Revolution. Even the passage of the first private express law in 1792—and its modifications since then—failed to stop the operators of the private expresses. In 1845, the report of the postmaster general, in language colorful enough to have come from any nineteenth century robber baron, described competitors as "plunderers of the public revenues."

Private entrepreneurs not only widely flouted the Private Express Statutes, but they apparently were also responsible for extending service into the more sparsely populated regions. According to Scheele,

> Private express lines were a principal feature of western communications during the early period of settling the Far West. While the government provided mail service on "principal routes," the express companies offered supplemental and rival service over such lines as, for example, the Nicaraguan Route. As the adventurous miners moved over the hills and mountains, the express operators followed quickly to maintain service between the camps and isolated towns and the nearest post office. The carriage of letters, gold dust, newspapers, and parcels was a lucrative business—undoubtedly more dependable than prospecting itself. Such express services were offered by both individuals or small organizations as well as the large national companies such as the Adams, American, National, and Wells Fargo concerns.
>
> In many respects, the most dramatic visions of the American postal service are associated with the words "Pony Express." The western pony express, however, was not a service originally established by the United States Post Office Department.[1]

Thus, the "pony express" now used to symbolize the Postal Service takes its original inspiration from private entrepreneurs, the firm of Russell, Majors and Waddell. It may be noted that the unofficial (and more or less inapplicable) motto of the Post Office— "Neither snow, nor rain, nor heat, nor gloom of night stays these couriers from the swift completion of their appointed rounds"—is also nonoriginal. It is attributed to the Greek historian Herodotus (c. 430 B.C.), who thus described the mounted couriers used by King Xerxes of Persia.[2]

By 1860 the Post Office had managed to have Congress plug most of the loopholes in the Private Express Statutes. Since that time the emphasis has been on interpretation and enforcement rather than on legislative action. The Post Office's monopoly on letter mail has not been seriously challenged by any major competitor for some time.

Competition since 1940

In the past few decades competition has developed for carriage of non-letter mail such as parcels and advertising material. The Postal Service faces major competition from (1) United Parcel Service for parcels, (2) a number of recently started firms specializing in home delivery of advertising material, and (3) companies which have found that they can deliver bills more cheaply by using their own employees than by using the mails. Study of this competition—its service, its cost to the public, and its internal efficiency—provides information relevant to an evaluation of the postal monopoly.

United Parcel Service (UPS). Many private firms in the United States now accept small parcels for delivery. Among them are Greyhound Package Service, REA Express, and over 80,000 local and short-haul truckers, specialized carriers, and retail store delivery services. In the general handling and delivery of parcels, though, the Postal Service has but one major competitor, United Parcel Service.

> During the past 11 years, the brown-uniformed UPS delivery men, in their familiar dark brown vans have quadrupled their deliveries of packages weighing one to fifty pounds— to about 600 million deliveries annually. This year's volume will top last year's by about 10 percent. The Postal Service's comparable business plummeted during the same eleven years to about 498 million parcels from 800 million. (The service still delivers almost twice as many packages as UPS if library materials, catalogs, parcels weighing less than a pound and certain special items are included, but that total has been declining, too.)[3]

Factual comparisons of costs and efficiency between UPS and the Postal Service are difficult because relatively few data are available and because the two operations are not strictly comparable. For example, virtually all parcels that enter the UPS system are from the 165,000 business firms constituting its regular customers, and almost none originate from the general public. Because of this, parcels handled by UPS are, on average, better packaged than those handled by the Postal Service. Moreover, UPS has many large customers supplying it with a substantial volume from relatively concentrated sources. Both UPS and the Postal Service impose size and weight restrictions. UPS accepts only those parcels which weigh less than 50 pounds and have a girth less than 120 inches. Postal Service limits on packages mailed between first-class post offices are slightly smaller—40 pounds and an 84-inch girth.[4]

The Postal Service refers to the activities of UPS as "cream-skimming." According to *Business Week*, "cream-skimming is exactly what irritates postal officials the most. 'We have to ship Aunt Minnie's cookies to her grandchildren,' says one of them, 'even if she doesn't wrap them so well and if the kids live on top of a mountain. You don't get that kind of service out of UPS.'"[5]

Since UPS is an interstate carrier, it is regulated by the Interstate Commerce Commission (ICC) and by state regulatory authorities as well. It must be licensed to do business in each state it serves. Despite its growth and success, UPS has not yet achieved nationwide status. It is now licensed to serve all or part of forty-six states and the District of Columbia. It is still not licensed to operate in four states—Alaska, Hawaii, Montana and Utah—and in parts of other states. Thus there is no true nationwide competitor to the Postal Service.

Many observers believe that, even after allowing generously for its advantages, UPS is still a more efficient operation than the Postal Service. UPS has pioneered in mechanizing and containerizing the handling of parcels. Mechanization and containerization produce lower handling costs and much lower breakage rates. According to Postmaster General Elmer T. Klassen, "We damage five packages for every one that United Parcel does."[6]

With the advantages of mechanization, UPS can provide lower rates, better pick-up services, and faster deliveries than the Postal Service. In 1972 customers such as Avon Products, Inc., found that Postal Service rates averaged 9 cents per pound while UPS rates averaged only 7 to 7.5 cents per pound.[7]

Consistency and reliability are important aspects of delivery service. This fact has been seized upon by UPS, but apparently lost in the shuffle by the Postal Service. For example, according to Crandon Clark, general traffic manager for W. T. Grant Co., "UPS claims that 95 percent of all deliveries within 150 miles will be made the next day, and it's true. Their standard of 95 percent has real meaning. *They meet it consistently.*"[8] (Emphasis added.) A similar view is voiced by James Edler, transportation manager of American Greetings Corp. of Cleveland: "The Postal Service is quite capable of matching UPS delivery time, *but they don't match it consistently; you just never know when to expect a package to arrive.*"[9] (Emphasis added.)

The Postal Service is now attempting to retrieve some of the business lost to UPS. According to a *Wall Street Journal* report in December 1972, the Postal Service is installing mechanized package-sorting and distributing systems similar to those developed by UPS, and incorporating them in a $1 billion network of thirty-three bulk-mail processing centers scheduled to be in operation by 1976. It is claimed, moreover, that employees of the Postal Service no longer throw packages as though they were ex-officio members of the Harlem Globe Trotters. For the first time in the 180-year history of the Post Office, it is claimed that parcels marked "fragile" are being handled separately (and, one hopes, more gently than they used to be). The Postal Service has strengthened its sales force and is sending "customer service representatives" out to seek new business. On the other hand, the newspapers recently reported the case of a woman who reacted strongly when the postal clerk slammed a stamp on her fragile cookies, whereupon the clerk had the woman arrested and the cookies sent to the bomb squad.[10]

It appears that the chief way in which the general public is at a disadvantage in the competition between UPS and the Postal Service is that UPS is frequently not available to the average citizen who wants to send a parcel. The average citizen may feel that he has no practical alternative to the Postal Service no matter how high its rates, how slow its service, or how extensive its breakage. From a policy viewpoint it is important to realize that the cure would be to *extend* competition between UPS and the Postal Service (and permit competition from anyone else who wants to compete), not to restrict competition by extending the statutory monopoly of the Postal Service.

The Post Office has been in the parcel post business since 1921. It has had ample opportunity to improve its service, as well as to capitalize on possible economies of scale in handling parcels. The apparent results of its head start and long experience are obsolete handling methods, high costs, high breakage rates, and slow service. It remains to be seen whether the Postal Service, with its new organization, can improve upon this record.

The existence of UPS is now generally taken for granted. Few (if any) suggest "outlawing" UPS and absorbing it into the Postal Service to increase efficiency. Yet, paradoxically, this is precisely the argument that is made for retaining the Private Express Statutes and the Postal Service's monopoly on first-class mail.

Private Posts. More than a dozen private mail-delivery companies are reportedly competing successfully with the Postal Service for third-class mail. These firms specialize in delivering unaddressed advertising circulars to residences. According to *U.S. News & World Report,* "these private delivery firms are doing a booming business. The reason: Customers are reported to be turning to them for fast and reliable deliveries—at relatively low cost." [11]

Leonard Merewitz lists twelve private postal firms and notes that "most have offices in several cities by the nature of their business." [12] In alphabetical order, these twelve organizations are: American Courier Corporation, American Postal System, California Postal System, Consumer Communication Services, Continental Postal Services, Independent Postal Service of America, Loomis Courier Service, Pacific Postal Service, Private Postal Systems of America, Rocket Messenger Service, United Clearings, and West Coast Mail Service.

The Independent Postal Service of America (IPSA), founded in 1968 in Oklahoma City, is one of the largest firms in this field. By 1971 IPSA had fifty-three offices in nineteen states and one in Canada, 18,000 employees, and the ability to deliver material to seven million homes.[13] Other firms queried by *U.S. News & World Report* were able to deliver unaddressed material to an additional two to three million homes. These rapidly growing and profitable organizations plan to expand their services: they stress the importance of fast, low cost, consistent service. Postmaster General Klassen said in June 1973 that "there are a number of private mail companies around the country giving us real concern. But they're not really a threat and they can't use stamps." [14]

Several firms report successful deliveries to specific addresses and the capability of delivering other addressed mail such as magazines or Christmas cards.[15] Paul Eckelberry, president of Consumer Communications Corporation in Columbus, Ohio, "guarantees when an ad or circular will be delivered" and "reports his firm offers savings of 35 to 40 percent compared with Postal Service costs. A factor in those savings is held to be that advertisers do not have to attach address labels and bundle mail as they must do for the U.S. System." [16]

The Private Express Statutes do not give the Postal Service a monopoly over third-class direct mail advertising. Hence present attempts to charge "full cost" rates for third-class mail will undoubtedly create new residential delivery services to individuals—unless, of course, Congress takes specific action to prevent this from happening.

Employee Delivery Systems. Although the Private Express Statutes prohibit delivery of first-class letters for a fee, any organization may use its own full-time employees to deliver its own letters without violating the law. Postmaster General Klassen recently reported that "Many of our customers try to deliver their own bills and that sort of thing directly by messenger." [17] At least one large utility company, Virginia Electric & Power Company, notes that it is currently saving a substantial amount of money by delivering some of its monthly service bills by messenger. Its controller, Mr. M. J. Hornsby, has said:

> The increase in first class postage rates from 6 cents to 8 cents which occurred in May 1971, resulted in a substantial increase in our operating expenses. In an effort to offset as much as possible this increased cost, we inaugurated a system of hand-delivering our bills in certain metropolitan areas of the larger cities we serve. Regular full-time employees are used as bill-deliverers. We estimate the cost to be approximately 5 cents per bill which is substantially less than the 8 cents first class rate. This system is still in effect although the tight labor market in our operating area has made it difficult to employ as many bill-deliverers as we would like. We are prohibited by the Private Express Statutes from employing part-time or temporary help as bill-deliverers. To this extent it may be said that the Statutes have had some adverse effect on our operations. If it were not for the prohibition of employing part-time or temporary help for this work, we could use high school or college students to great advantage.

Mr. Hornsby also reported that the company provides its

> own courier service daily between several of our larger district offices and our main office for the transportation of first class material. It is quite possible that the repeal of the Private Express Statutes would encourage enterprising individuals to enter this type of business. The resulting competition could prove beneficial to all having a need for this service.[18]

Virginia Electric & Power started its own delivery service because the increase from six to eight cent postage would have added about $250,000 per year to its costs. Since the company can deliver a single item to individual customers for only five cents, first-class postal rates appear to contain so much "cream" that they invite extensive cream-skimming by do-it-yourselfers. In the future, as postal rates rise, more companies may take advantage of this exemption from the Private Express Statutes and start using their own employees to deliver their bills.[19]

Conclusions

In retrospect, it appears that such private postal competition as has existed from time to time has served the public interest well. For over 300 years would-be competitors have been pioneering innovations, reducing costs, and improving services.

For the past 100 years the Private Express Statutes have been rigorously enforced. This enforcement has at all times been based solely on evidence that monopolistic postal revenues—*not the public interest*—are harmed by the existence of vigorous competition.

Rigorous enforcement of the Private Express Statutes has clearly had a substantial impact on the nature of our existing delivery systems. With few exceptions, pioneering attempts at private delivery have been quashed and are no longer in existence. One can only guess at how many private carriers would exist today, how large they would be, or how much better our delivery service would be if our laws did not grant the Post Office such an effective monopoly.

CHAPTER III

FUTURE COMPETITION

The persistence of the statutory postal monopoly on letter mail makes it difficult to form an idea of what life might be like if the Postal Service were to face comprehensive competition for all kinds of mail service. To make it easier to form that idea, this chapter examines the nature of competition for postal services.

The fact is that every monopolist, no matter how secure his monopoly, has some competition. The Post Office is no exception. Throughout its history it has faced a number of competitive challenges. In parcel post, for example, it has lost ground steadily to United Parcel Service. However, when competition has threatened to take away letter mail, the Post Office has prevailed by resorting to legislative or legal action. But if the Private Express Statutes should be repealed, the Postal Service would then have to command public support solely on the basis of the speed, regularity, dependability, and economy of the service which it provides. This, to put it mildly, would cause it some problems.

Even if the Private Express Statutes are not repealed, the Postal Service will be faced with increased competition. The policy choice regarding future operating conditions for the Postal Service is not between competition or no competition. Rather, as will be seen, the real policy question is whether the Postal Service should be forced to face more or less competition. Since the Postal Service must already compete in many areas, repeal of the Private Express Statutes would by no means open an entirely new ball game. However, repeal and the threat of increased competition would force the Postal Service to be more responsive to the needs of the public.

To help focus on the source and nature of competition it should be recognized that the Postal Service is an important part of the communications and shipping industries. The delivery of letters, magazines, newspapers, and advertising puts it in the communications industry, and parcel post puts it in the shipping industry. Just as technological developments such as television have caused certain magazines (for example, *Life*) to become obsolete, so other technological developments can make physical transmission of the mails obsolete.

The milieu in which the Postal Service operates is not static. A substantial number of changes are already either well under way or may be confidently predicted. As a means of isolating the probable effect of terminating the statutory monopoly, future possibilities will be discussed under two headings: (1) the kind of competition likely to occur if the Postal Service continues on its present course, assuming that the Private Express Statutes *are not repealed,* and (2) the competition that the Post Office will face, assuming the Private Express Statutes *are repealed.*

Future Competition under the Private Express Statutes

Even if the Postal Service had no competitors at all, continually increasing postal rates would be likely to produce protective reactions from postal customers. When Congress established the independent U.S. Postal Service, it provided legislative guidelines for raising rates on second- and third-class mail (newspapers or periodicals and advertising) so that revenues from these sources would cover the "directly attributable" costs of handling this mail plus a fair share of all "nonattributable" costs.[1] The most dramatic impact of these rate increases will fall on newspapers and magazines (second-class mail). Obviously, the more frequently a magazine is published, the greater will be the financial impact of increased postal rates. The impact on weekly magazines will be four times greater than that on monthlies of comparable circulation.

Distribution of Newspapers and Magazines (Second-class Mail). Assuming that rate increases for newspapers and magazines take place as planned, publishers will move to minimize the impact on their distribution costs. Six possible short-run cost-reducing alternatives which publishers may adopt are:

(1) Magazines or newspapers can be printed on lighter-weight paper; overseas editions of British newspapers are always printed on lightweight paper.

(2) Smaller formats can be adopted. *Fortune* magazine, for example, recently made such a change in order to reduce transportation costs.

(3) Electronic transmission of printing plates coupled with regional multiple printing is another means of reducing transportation costs. Many magazines do this already, but increased postal rates will accelerate the practice.

(4) Magazines can be transported by private trucks and mailed at the post office of final destination. This practice will reduce a portion of the handling and cost attributable to and charged for by the Postal Service.

(5) Frequency of publication can be decreased. For example, some weekly magazines can be published biweekly or semimonthly instead.

(6) Publishers can increase their sales through newstands or magazine stores. In England virtually all magazines are said to be distributed this way, with virtually none being delivered by the British Post Office.

These alternatives are immediately available to publishers. Some are already being used; others are in the process of being adopted. Publishers turning to any of these alternatives will reduce their expenses and, at the same time, will reduce the revenues of the Postal Service. The last four alternatives will also reduce the physical volume of mail flowing into and clogging the postal system. While these alternatives do not involve the establishment of direct competitors to the Postal Service, they force the Postal Service to reckon with problems similar to those posed by competition.

Looking beyond these six possibilities, one finds it entirely conceivable that when the full impact of postal rates increases is felt— when rates have been raised to "full cost"—publishers will seek (and someone will offer) private, independent delivery service in metropolitan and suburban areas. No particular prescience is required to foresee that publishers will be on the lookout for cheaper alternatives, since postage represents a substantial expense to most magazine publishers. The Private Express Statutes do not apply to second-class mail, and there are no other legal restrictions to preclude anyone from offering a private delivery service.

Alternate delivery services for magazines are at present almost nonexistent. But if history is any guide, it is certain that competition will arise as soon as someone finds it profitable to compete. Unless entry into a potentially profitable situation is artificially suppressed, competitors will spring up like weeds in the springtime. At least three distinct possibilities come to mind. First, in many metropolitan areas the local newspaper is delivered daily by regular carriers. In order to earn a little extra money, newspapers might agree to have their carriers deliver magazines as well. Second, in many areas there are organizations whose representatives regularly sell magazine subscriptions on a door-to-door basis. It is entirely conceivable that publishers may prevail upon these same organizations to add magazine deliveries to their salesmen's tasks. In this way, a new form of service organization could evolve. Third, magazine publishers may turn to the new firms that have been formed to deliver third-class mail. As rates for second-class mail are raised to full cost, magazine publishers may join with these firms in developing new home delivery services.

These possibilities of course assume that some energetic private entrepreneurs will believe they can deliver magazines to subscribers more cheaply or more rapidly than the Postal Service and still earn a profit (after payment of local and federal taxes, from which the Postal Service is exempt). However, if the Postal Service can do the job better, more cheaply, and more rapidly than anyone else, then it need not fear competition, even though it charges full cost. It should be realized, however, that it has not been Post Office efficiency, but rather the subsidization of second-class rates, which has precluded anyone from offering an alternative delivery service. If the Private Express Statutes are not repealed, then the Postal Service may continue to use profits from first-class mail to subsidize second-class mail, thereby precluding possible competition.[2] This practice is clearly contrary to stated public policy in all areas of private endeavor. Any large industrial firm which engaged in such predatory practices would be subject to vigorous antitrust prosecution by the Justice Department. If the policy is a good one for the private sector, it would be sensible to apply it to the Post Office too.

Direct Mail Advertising (Third-class Mail). Postal rates for advertising matter are already inducing a number of private firms to offer alternate delivery service. As these rates are raised still higher, it is reasonable to expect that existing private delivery firms will grow and that still more firms will be inspired to enter the business. It is possible that, in time, much of the direct mail advertising matter will be distributed by private post.

Parcels (Fourth-class Mail). Generally the Postal Service has higher rates, more breakage, and slower and less dependable service than its principle competitor, United Parcel Service. The Postal Service hopes that by 1980 its $1 billion construction program for modern mechanized facilities will enable it to be as efficient as UPS. Insufficient evidence exists for determining whether the Postal Service will achieve this goal—but it may be noted that in the past most attempts to mechanize and improve productivity have failed to live up to the promises which had previously flowed from widespread public relations campaigns. However, because of competition from United Parcel and others, it is certain that the Postal Service cannot generate a fiscal surplus from parcel post for subsidization of other classes of mail.[3]

Developments in Electronic Communications. By now it should be apparent that competition to the Postal Service is not only thinkable, but already exists. The story does not end here, however. Competitive entrepreneurs can be expected to reach into every area not firmly and absolutely protected by law. Competitive economic forces ordinarily show little respect for time-honored traditions or institutions, especially when they are inefficient. We may conclude by mentioning two other important sources of potential competition: development of the "checkless society" and electronic facsimile transmission.

Items such as bills or charge account statements, monthly payments to utilities, credit cards, social security checks, and dividend checks constitute a substantial portion of first-class mail. Computer manufacturers and banks are endeavoring to develop, by means of solid-state electronic technology, a cashless-checkless society. This means the Postal Service may soon find itself competing indirectly with computer firms like IBM. If banks and computer manufacturers succeed in developing even a portion of such a system, the Postal Service will be threatened with the loss of a significant portion of its first-class mail volume, and the current Private Express Statutes will be powerless to prevent the resulting loss of revenue.[4]

The second potentially important development comes from Xerox and the other manufacturers of electronic copying equipment who are attempting to develop low-cost means of facsimile transmission to be used in conjunction with the telephone. The basic technology is already developed and is now offered commercially, but its cost is too high to be competitive with the mails. Further advances in solid-state technology could lower costs and change the picture significantly.

Summary. In conclusion, the current Private Express Statutes are capable of protecting the volume of mail and postal revenues only up to a point. First-class rates are now so high that utility firms are being encouraged to use their own employees to deliver monthly bills.[5] In the past a major barrier to effective competition for second-

and third-class mail has been the continued willingness of Congress to provide publishers and direct mail advertisers with substantial subsidies, partly from the general Treasury and partly from first-class mail. In the one area where the Post Office has historically attempted to recover full cost (parcel post rates), major competition has flourished and is now regarded by most observers as providing lower rates, better pickup service, and less breakage.

The Postal Service already exists in a whirlpool of competitive economic forces. In this milieu its dominant position is protected as much by government subsidy and tax forgiveness as by the Private Express Statutes. An attempt to become fully self-sufficient by recovering total cost (exclusive of taxes) over all types of mail would put the Postal Service to a severe competitive challenge.

Competitive Developments if the Private Express Statutes Are Repealed

Termination of the statutory monopoly would only increase the competitive pressures facing the Post Office. This section examines the underlying economic forces that would influence likely outcomes in the event Congress were to repeal the Private Express Statutes.

Outright repeal would expose all first-class mail to *potential* competition. However, repeal by itself would not be sufficient to cause competition to materialize. Competition will arise only when private entrepreneurs are reasonably convinced that they can earn a profit from their enterprise. In order to attract business, any new competitor will either have to deliver mail at rates lower than Postal Service rates or provide better service at existing rates. In either case, he must keep his operating costs (including taxes) below those of the Postal Service (which does not pay taxes) in order to earn the necessary profit.

The profit motive will naturally lead private entrepreneurs to introduce cost-saving innovations. It will also lead them to subdivide first-class mail and look for those portions which have lower-than-average handling costs or which demand a kind of service the Postal Service does not provide. This process of subdividing mail into different cost categories and then serving only the more profitable (lower cost) categories is referred to by monopolists as "cream-skimming."

The historic battle cry of the Post Office is that, given repeal of the Private Express Statutes, private competitors would skim off the most profitable part of the mail, leaving the government with unprofitable skim milk. The Post Office readily acknowledges that private firms would indeed give some users a better deal, but it argues that taxpayers or other mail users would be forced to pay more to make up the resulting deficit. This argument constitutes a major bulwark in defense of the Private Express Statutes and must be critically examined.[6]

Cream-skimming. By way of introduction, it should be recognized that when postal authorities argue that private firms will skim the cream, their argument demonstrates a recognition that cream is there to be skimmed. In other words, some mail users are overcharged under the existing rate structure. In a truly competitive market, these rate-making practices would be self-defeating. In a competitive market, cream-skimmers are the "good guys" who protect consumer interests by keeping other suppliers honest. In a market without sufficient competition, the consumer is overcharged. Cream-skimmers are thus the backbone of the free enterprise system: an abundance of such competitors is good insurance that Adam Smith's "invisible hand" will cause the market to function in the public interest rather than for enhancement of private interests.

If a market is less than fully competitive and if competitors resort to collusion in order to inject more monopolistic profits ("cream") into their revenue, these practices are considered predatory, exploitative, and against the public interest. Hence, "creaming" a market is typically against public policy and is subject to prosecution under our antitrust laws. The subject of cream-skimming tends to arise only in markets in which a recognized monopoly exists or which have been subjected to illegal restraint of trade.[7]

In order to understand this subject more fully, it is necessary to know which portions of the postal system represent cream and which represent skim milk. Some mail delivered by the Post Office has a cost which exceeds the revenues attributable to it. This is the skim milk. The Postal Service claims that it needs excess profits ("cream") on some mail in order to compensate for losses on other mail. Losses attributable to delivery of newspapers and magazines represent probably the best known subsidy and the one most widely discussed in debates on postal rates. Delivery of this mail at deliberately low rates resulted in losses which were not reimbursable through explicit appropriations for public service subsidies and which therefore had to be compensated from other sources of revenue, that is, general appropriations and profits on first-class mail.

In addition to low rates for newspapers and magazines, in the past the rate structure also contained deliberate subsidies to libraries and educational and nonprofit organizations. Discounts given to these institutions were part of a recognized "public service" subsidy which in the past Congress explicitly appropriated as such from general tax revenues. Under the law creating the Postal Service, most of these deliberate subsidies are due to be gradually lowered.

In other words, part of the annual deficit of the Postal Service is incurred by knowingly and deliberately setting some rates below cost. This part of the loss is covered by a "revenue foregone" subsidy appropriated annually by Congress. The remainder of the deficit may be attributed to costs rising more rapidly than anticipated, to delays in approving rate increases, or to low rates which Congress would neither raise nor supplement with an explicit subsidy. Obviously, it is not necessary for first-class mail to generate surplus revenues to subsidize mail already provided with a subsidy through congressional appropriations.

Another portion of the annual public service subsidy is for rural (RFD) routes. It is widely recognized that the costs of serving sparsely settled rural routes canot be covered by the standard prevailing postage rates. Many of these routes would show a loss even if the total revenue from all mail delivered on such routes were assigned to cover the costs of the rural carriers. Consequently, if provision of rural mail services were not subsidized (which is unlikely and which is certainly not advocated here), then either rural service would have to be curtailed, or postage rates to rural addresses would have to be increased, or rural boxholders would have to pay an annual fee to insure delivery at normal postage rates.

In order to avoid taxing other categories of mail, Congress has established the principle that it will appropriate general tax revenues to subsidize delivery service on rural routes. Hence, these extra costs need not be subsidized by profits on other first-class mail.

Other High-cost Delivery Routes. The high cost of delivering mail on sparsely settled rural routes is but the tip of the well-known iceberg. Variation in delivery costs is far more extensive than is generally realized.

The cost of delivering mail varies widely, and depends to a large degree on the extent of service which the Postal Service provides. For example, among suburban households many existing carrier routes are "curb routes"— routes on which a motor vehicle is used to deliver the mail to a familiar curb-side mailbox. However, in many older residential areas, mail is still delivered to the front porch or front door: since the carrier usually walks these routes, they are known within the Postal Service as "foot routes." Delivery to the front door, on foot, clearly constitutes better service and costs the Postal Service more per household than curb delivery.

Low-cost Delivery. Delivery to large apartment houses is less expensive than either "curb routes" or "foot routes." The Postal Service will only deliver mail to one physical location at each residential address, and apartment houses are therefore required to provide banks of mailboxes for the residents somewhere in the lobby area. Thus with one stop mail is delivered economically to dozens or hundreds of households at one time. Some large urban apartment houses even have a deskman who sorts all mail for tenants: for the Postal Service this means the carrier need only drop a mailbag at the desk and continue on his route.

From the Postal Service's point of view, probably the most lucrative of all forms of delivery is mail addressed to "P.O. Box No. ..". This mail is easily sorted into the appropriate box without its leaving the post office. In addition to the advantages of the low cost of delivery, the Postal Service also receives a rental fee for the box.

As a result of these wide variations in delivery cost, it is clear that many households receive an implicit subsidy from the Postal Service. There is an implicit discrimination in favor of people who live in houses (and who receive individual delivery service), and against apartment dwellers (who are denied delivery to the door of their apartment).

Because of these differences in delivery costs and because a far higher proportion of apartment houses are in cities than in suburban or rural areas, the Postal Service systematically discriminates against cities and in favor of suburbs. Postmaster General Klassen has admitted that, within the postal operation, the cities routinely subsidize the suburbs.[8] To some extent, then, the Postal Service is playing a reverse Robin Hood, taking from the poorer central cities in order to help the more affluent suburbs.

Low-cost Letter Mail. First-class mail received at the Post Office for sorting and delivery varies significantly in cost and ease of delivery. Some portion of letter mail is composed of individually typed business letters, personal checks in payment of charge accounts, handwritten letters from Aunt Tillie, postcards, wedding announcements, invitations, or thank-you notes. This certainly is not all cream, and some of it may indeed be skim milk. To take an extreme illustration, consider the occasional postcard or letter dropped into a mailbox at some out-of-the-way place in Hawaii for delivery to, say, Boothbay Harbor, Maine. The cost involved in sorting and processing this particular item before it arrives at its final destination will far exceed the postage.[9]

The real cream in today's postal system is what is best described (unofficially) as "bulk" first-class mail. This is mail mass-produced by computer—bills from utility companies, department stores, or charge cards, as well as monthly bank statements, brokerage statements, and so on. With relatively little extra effort on the part of the mailers, the computer can be programmed to print statements by order of the ZIP code. With a little additional effort the computer can even arrange the mail by individual carrier route. Since all items are of uniform size, they can easily be bundled together at the source. A significant part of all first-class mail falls into this category.

It should be noted that these efficiencies and the resulting savings in distribution costs are generated by the mailer and not by the Postal Service. In spite of the economies inherent in their operation, these users are being charged unnecessarily high rates for using the mails—costs which must of course be passed on to their own customers.

Although the Postal Service reaps the benefits and achieves large "savings" or "profits" in processing and delivering presorted first-class mail, it would be wrong to infer from this fact that the postal system itself generates any economies of scale. As we shall discover later, economies of scale in the Postal Service are by no means certain.

Future Competition. The nature of the competition that would follow repeal of the Private Express Statutes can be forecast with some assurance. The allegation that private postal firms would cater to those discriminated against by the present rate structure is almost surely correct. This means that, in the beginning at least, competitors (1) would have a strong tendency to confine their delivery services to relatively dense or easily serviced routes, and (2) within those areas where they deliver, would solicit mail principally or exclusively from large establishments whose mail is already presorted and ready for immediate distribution.[10]

Competitors would also attempt to offer business firms services which the Postal Service was unable or unwilling to provide. An investigation and report by the Inspection Service of the U.S. Postal Service made the following observations:

> The violations which warrant greatest concern are those stimulated by the desire for better service. . . .
> Wide area collections, coupled with rapid distribution and dispatch for delivery early the next morning within a radius of about 200 miles, have become the basis for transfer of business from the Postal Service to couriers by food, drug and department store chain operators. Their payroll, pricing, accounting, inventory and supply processes are bene-

fitted so much by the overnight service that cost becomes secondary.[11]

The report further noted that "existing services can be improved simultaneously with the development of new products." Thus, as has happened repeatedly throughout the history of the postal monopoly, the Postal Service has left gaps which private entrepreneurs would doubtless fill if they were permitted to do so.

It is more difficult to tell the extent to which private competitors would succeed. If the Private Express Statutes were repealed, the Postal Service could make competitive efforts to save this choice business for itself. It already has an advantage in its tax exemption. Furthermore, nothing in the existing law prevents the Postal Service from taking preemptive action and doing what private competitors will sooner or later force it to do anyhow. To be more specific, it costs substantially less to deliver mail that has been presorted by computer, and the Postal Service could well afford to offer "bulk first-class" discounts similar to discounts for bulk third-class mail. This suggestion has been made before.[12] It is of interest to note that the Postal Service has such a proposal on file before the Postal Rate Commission—that it is already moving to establish in its rate structure a principle which would be forced upon it if free and open competition were permitted.[13]

If the Postal Service improves its existing services, offers needed new services, and is alert in its pricing policies (and if it can achieve economies of scale), then no serious or important competitors would arise even if the Private Express Statutes were repealed. On the other hand, if the Postal Service is slow to react, or if economies of scale turned out to be more ephemeral than real, then vigorous competition would be likely to arise in most urban centers, despite the tax exemption enjoyed by the Postal Service.

Conclusions

Postal competition, where it exists, serves the consumer's interest well. For third- and fourth-class mail, private firms now offer cheaper and more expeditious service than that provided by the Postal Service.

In response to this competition, the Postal Service is attempting to improve the way it handles parcels and to expedite delivery of dated fourth-class mail. Existing competition is also benefiting the Postal Service. Since recent growth in mail volume has frequently been too rapid for the Postal Service to handle, it is indeed fortunate that competition for third- and fourth-class mail has developed with sufficient speed to prevent the Postal Service from being choked any more than it already is.

The existence of alternative providers of first-class mail service would almost surely have similar salutary effects on service, and lead to cost reductions as well. Repealing the Private Express Statutes would probably result in great improvement of mail service during periods such as Christmas, when the Postal Service is clogged by unusually high volumes of mail. Private firms now providing third-class mail delivery have offered to handle Christmas first-class mail. If they were allowed to do so, peak loads on the Postal Service would be reduced, service deterioration at such times would no longer be customary and, since peak volume is especially costly, the Postal Service's cost performance would probably improve.

A second and important consequence of repeal would be to force rates to levels somewhat more consistent with costs (except for those categories of service subsidized annually by Congress) and to reduce the overcharging of some users of first-class mail. A third beneficial consequence would be the development of specialized services to meet special needs not now served by the Postal Service.

CHAPTER IV

POLICY ISSUES

Certainly historical precedent does not constitute good reason for continuing the statutory postal monopoly. The fundamental policy question is whether the monopoly bestows benefits on society (and secondarily whether these benefits, if any, are sufficient to merit retention of the monopoly). To put it another way, what would be the advantages and disadvantages of the extra competition that would result if the Postal Service were deprived of its statutory monopoly?

It will be remembered from the previous chapter that the Postal Service will face increased competition from a number of sources even if Congress does not repeal the Private Express Statutes. This competition will divert some mail and revenue from the Postal Service. However, because these results will occur regardless of repeal, their desirability is not germane to the present discussion.

What is important are those advantages or disadvantages which would accrue *only if there is repeal*. The following sections first discuss the economic advantages and disadvantages of repeal and then consider other pertinent (but noneconomic) questions.

Economic Considerations

The principal economic issue raised by the postal monopoly concerns economies of scale, or the extent to which unit cost decreases as output increases. This subject is discussed below and in the Appendix. To summarize the discussion, it may be said that the existence of economies of scale does not, in itself, provide any economic justification for a statutory postal monopoly. Empirical evidence on economies of scale is not necessarily pertinent to policy issues concerning repeal of the statutory postal monopoly.[1] In fact, if economies of scale are such as to create a natural monopoly, there is no need for a statutory monopoly. Since these economies would enable the Postal Service to undermine its competitors, it would not need protection against the development of competition.

Economies of Scale. The chief economic question raised by economies of scale, if they in fact exist, is the rates that ought to be charged for various mail services. That is, assuming that mail services (and users of those services) are to be separated into certain rate categories, what rate structure would represent a fair and equitable sharing of nonattributable costs? In particular, should rates be set competitively?

Evidence concerning the existence of economies of scale is sometimes believed to be important to the question whether the Post Office ought to have a statutory monopoly. This belief is mistaken. In fact, the existence or nonexistence of economies of scale is essentially irrelevant to the fundamental policy issue. Since the available evidence is inconclusive, it is fortunate that it is mostly irrelevant. (A review of such empirical evidence as does exist is contained in the Appendix.)

What many fail to recognize is that even if the postal system does constitute a natural monopoly, this in no way provides any economic justification for "sanctifying" the situation by statute. In other words, a natural monopolist can *by definition* operate at such low cost as to preclude competition without further assistance from the government. In plain English, a natural monopolist does not need a legal monopoly. Conferring a statutory monopoly on a natural monopoly serves only to exaggerate monopoly power. The policy issue created by the existence of natural monopoly is not how to protect the monopolist, but how to protect the public from being exploited by the monopolist. The conclusion is that the statutory monopoly conferred by the existing Private Express Statutes has no economic justification regardless of whether economies of scale exist. Alfred Marshall, the English economist, clearly recognized the lack of any economic justification for continuance of the legal monopoly.

> If the state, with its enormous advantage for this particular business, can be undersold by private competitors, the reason must be either that it is extending its claim to the possession of business in regions where its special advantages fail, and where, therefore, there is no good reason for having the work done by a government department with or without a monopoly, or else that it shows a grievous want of enterprise. It is idle to lay stress on the need of keeping up the Post Office Revenue. For that part of the revenue which is reaped by the State as a result of its possessing the econ-

omies of production on a large scale would not be appreciably affected by the loss of its monopoly; and this is the only part of the revenue which is capable of being defended for a moment on economic grounds.[2]

Marshall may have erred in his presumption that the state has "enormous advantages for this particular business." History does not demonstrate that the state has any particular flair for excelling at mail delivery, nor do empirical studies suggest the existence of any economies of scale. The historical record shows merely that the state has been able at some cost to maintain a postal system and deliver the mail. However, except for Marshall's mistaken presumption that the government possesses some undefined (and likely enough nonexistent), "enormous" comparative advantage, his economic analysis is flawless.

It is important that this argument be fully understood by those interested in formulating public policy on the Private Express Statutes. Let us consider a specific illustration from our present postal system.

It is generally agreed that one particular component of the postal system, delivery to sparsely settled RFD routes, contains more elements of natural monopoly than any other part of the postal system. Deliveries are accomplished at a relatively high cost per unit, and RFD carriers ordinarily have substantial excess capacity. That is, with relatively little extra effort and at very little additional cost, they could deliver substantially more mail.[3] It would probably be wasteful and socially undesirable for anyone to duplicate service on these rural routes. Widespread recognition of this fact is consistent with the presumption that rural mail routes represent a natural monopoly. Equally consistent is the fact that no private competitor seems likely to start a competing mail service in these areas.[4] In other words, the Postal Service does not need the Private Express Statutes to protect its rural routes, which are its principal natural monopoly. Nor does the public interest require the Private Express Statutes to prevent socially undesirable investment from creating further excess capacity along rural routes.

What the Postal Service rightly fears is competition in the densely populated areas where unit cost is lower and the existence of any economies of scale dubious. In other words, the Postal Service does not require statutory protection for those isolated components which represent natural monopoly; rather, it requires protection for its "unnatural" monopoly. But surely government protection of an unnatural monopoly is undesirable.

Postal Technology. The irrelevance of economies of scale to the question of retention of the Private Express Statutes seems evident. Nevertheless, practical men will ask the legitimate question: What might go wrong if the Private Express Statutes are repealed? The Postal Service maintains that its monopoly is socially efficient and that competition for letter mail among different postal services would be wasteful.[5] To support this position the postal authorities have on occasion cited incorrect and misleading analogies between postal technology and public utilities. The purpose of this section is to discuss some important distinguishing characteristics of postal technology and provide practical answers to questions about what could go wrong.

Today's postal technology embodies some economic characteristics that are important in consideration of repeal. For example, most of the resources in a postal system are highly transferable. Postal "technology" consists chiefly of people: despite all efforts at mechanization, 80 to 85 percent of all costs are still labor-related. The remaining 15 to 20 percent of postal costs are for the purchase of (1) transportation services from airlines, truckers, and railroads, (2) trucks and delivery vehicles, (3) facilities and (4) specialized mail-handling equipment. Investment in specialized capital equipment designed exclusively for postal operations is low. The resulting economic situation contrasts sharply with that of public utilities such as pipelines where a major share of costs is for specialized equipment.

To illustrate this distinction, let us suppose that policy is designed to force the installation of multiple, small, inefficient pipelines along the same route and serving the same customers. The resulting inefficiencies would be great because economies of scale would be lost and because the resources invested in pipeline construction are irrevocably committed for the life of the pipeline, which could be as long as forty to fifty years. Thus, in legislative decisions concerning pipelines, a mistaken presumption in favor of encouraging multiple competitors and preventing economically scaled operations from competing for the business could embody high implicit social costs.

The technology of pipelines is, however, far closer to a "natural" monopoly than is that of the postal system.[6] High sunk costs are most certainly not a feature of postal technology. This distinction is important for policy purposes. It means that analogies between the postal system and other public utilities are apt to be false and misleading. The low investment costs required by postal technology suggest that the cost of presumptive error in favor of postal competition is negligible, while the potential gain from experimentation and increased efficiency is high. In other words, repeal of the Private Express Statutes in order to permit postal competition is almost surely correct public policy. If by any chance repeal should turn out to be a mistake, unprofitable private posts could disband and the resources (mostly labor and delivery vehicles) could be quickly and readily transferred to other productive uses in the economy. The sunk costs of any specialized equipment which might have to be written off would be small.

Competitive Rate-making. The Postal Service argues that the Private Express Statutes should be kept in effect because postal operations realize sufficient economies of scale to constitute a natural monopoly.[7] As Alfred Marshall observed, natural monopoly neither requires nor deserves statutory protection. Marshall favored removing statutory protection and permitting actual or potential competition to limit the rates which the Post Office could charge. In other words, Marshall favored what might be described as "competitively determined" rates, even if the Post Office continued to be the sole supplier of postal services.

The question which deserves careful consideration is this: would the public interest be harmed if the Postal Service were to establish a rate structure designed to make it self-sufficient and yet preclude competition? In other words, what would happen if (1) the Postal Service were stripped of its statutory monopoly and (2) it then decided that, in order to preclude competitors from rushing in and skimming its monopolistic cream, it would reduce rates on those classes of mail which can be delivered at a low unit cost? In other words, in order to prevent cream-skimming, the Postal Service might elect to charge less on those selected classes of letter mail now being gouged by the existing monopolistic rate structure.

Lowering rates on those selected categories of first-class mail which are highly lucrative would, other things being equal, increase the postal deficit and force the Postal Service to look elsewhere for increased revenues. One possibility would be to raise rates on other mail, either on other "miscellaneous" first-class mail not subject to discounts or on other classes of mail. This would be in keeping with the idea of levying all charges on the sender.[8] The main possibility here is that of raising rates on the first- or third-class mail least subject to competition. It is likely that viable competition would force the Postal Service to adopt some variant of this approach.

The Postal Service just breaks even on parcel post (fourth-class mail) even though it is tax exempt and its rates are substantially higher than those of the United Parcel Service. On second-class rates the Postal Service ostensibly loses money. Since it would have to overcome highly organized and highly vocal opposition in order to increase these rates to the point where it broke even, it has little likelihood of earning a profit on second-class mail and using this profit to subsidize "other" first-class mail.

Thus, by a process of elimination, if the Postal Service is to be competitive *and self-sustaining*, it must either increase its efficiency,[9] raise the rates on "other" first- or third-class mail, or levy a charge on some recipients (as it does for postal-box holders) for systematic differences in the "quality" of delivery service, where "quality" is related to cost.[10] Although this last course breaks with tradition, it is the most obvious way for the Postal Service to rationalize its rate structure, preclude competition and maintain its dominant position.

The net result of the restructuring of rates that would follow repeal of the Private Express Statutes would be that those first-class users who are now being grossly overcharged would pay lower rates, while those users of other classes of mail who are now paying too little would be charged somewhat more. In short, a competitive pricing structure would more nearly approximate the equitable result of various users and classes of mail paying for the cost of their own service.

What is likely to happen if rates are not competitively determined? The Postal Rate Commission has completed its first formal set of hearings on postal rates and has handed down its first decisions. The reasoning used in the first set of hearings contains an implicit bias against first-class mailers. This bias arose when the examiner decided that the elasticity of demand (the reaction of users to an increase in price) was an important factor in determining what share of nonattributable costs should be borne by each class of mail. So long as the Postal Service has a statutory monopoly over letter mail, the demand confronting the Postal Service for this service will be much more inelastic than the demand for other classes of mail. If the Private Express Statutes were repealed, however, the demand for first-class mail service from the Postal Service would, in short order, become much more elastic. So long as Congress continues the statutory monopoly, it has implicitly legislated higher rates for first-class mail.

Increased Efficiency. The analysis and discussion in the preceding section assumed that the postal system was operating as efficiently as possible under present conditions—as efficiently as it could operate, not as efficiently as a competitor could operate. Of course, potential but unrealized efficiencies might lower unit costs dramatically.[11] Since competition has been systematically suppressed, one can only speculate as to whether competitive forces would produce economies and savings. Such speculation is, however, pertinent to the question of the possible effects of the Private Express Statutes.

In an enterprise where over 80 percent of all costs are wage-related, it would appear that room exists for substantial improvement. The Postal Service and its predecessor have undertaken a number of design studies and experiments aimed at mechanization. Yet labor costs have remained at about 80 percent of total cost for many years. It is not clear why these research and development efforts have not produced better results. What the postal system may need is a stronger incentive or at least a shining example of how to do the job better. Competition from the private sector can be counted on to provide the incentive for undertaking innovative experiments, which could lead in time to better methods. History has repeatedly witnessed this pattern, from Dockwra's penny post and Povey's bell-ringers down to the mechanized parcel sorting system developed by United Parcel Service.

Containerization and mechanization of mail handling is a good illustration of a specific technological area which has not been adequately explored by the Postal Service. The familiar mailbag traces its origins back at least to the time of the Phoenicians when it was used to save "cube" (space) on tiny sailing vessels. Today mailbags are still used to save cube. However, unloading an entire rail car or airplane full of mailbags is without question one of the more labor-intensive—and backbreaking—jobs left in our industrial society. Despite the many advances in fork-lift trucks and mechanized handling technology, the Post Office's chief accomplishment over the last 200 years has been limited to the introduction of durable, lightweight, colored nylon bags for use with airmail. In the shipping of parcels it is interesting to note that United Parcel Service has containerized much of its operation, whereas the Postal Service continues to ship all parcels in bags. It would appear that in order to minimize cube, today's postal system is maximizing breakage and handling costs. In the area of containerization and mechanization, it is reasonable to conclude that free competition could not have resulted in less innovation. Further, because so much room is left for improvement, competition might accomplish a great deal in improving technology, reducing costs and lightening the burden on overworked mail handlers.

Finally, it should be noted that proponents of a gargantuan postal establishment neglect the possibility that a number of smaller and more highly specialized facilities might turn out to be more efficient. For example, if private firms specializing in magazine delivery handled all magazines, they might develop equipment or procedures to greatly facilitate that process. Similarly, it might be far more efficient to establish specialized facilities to handle nothing but bulk presorted letter mail than to continue to process this mail in conjunction with other mail. These few suggestions obviously do not exhaust the possibilities for improvement.

In conclusion, it is not at all clear that today's postal monopoly represents maximum efficiency. There are reasons for believing that active competition will produce innovations that will simultaneously improve service and lower costs.

Practical Realities

It would be folly to expect that important policy issues can be settled solely on the basis of economic reasoning about cream-skimming or economies of scale. The real world includes personalities, human emotions, uncertainties and other dynamic factors which must all be taken into account.

While it is not possible to address all the questions which might be raised about the postal monopoly, two particular issues are worth special attention—(1) postal strikes and labor relations and (2) incentives governing management of the postal system.

Postal Strikes. The right of postal workers to organize and to bargain collectively is now well established, but laws regulating the right of any government employee to strike are in a state of flux. At present, federal law does not allow strikes by public employees, including postal workers. Laws of some states permit state employees to strike, whereas laws of other states do not. Generally the trend is in the direction of giving public employees the right to strike, and it is not unreasonable to expect that postal unions will obtain this right in time.

In the case of a telephone industry strike, the highly automated nature of the telephone system makes it possible, with the aid of supervisory employees, for virtually all emergency calls (and most other calls as well) to be completed without delay. The situation is different in the case of the labor-intensive Postal Service. Given the existing postal monopoly, a legally permitted postal strike would disrupt all first-class mail service in the United States, and possibly no mail whatsoever would move. During an unofficial and unauthorized eight-day strike in New York in 1970, the National Guard had to be mobilized to deliver the mail.

The United Kingdom has also suffered unauthorized postal strikes. On one occasion, in 1964, the U.K. experienced a complete tie-up of the mails because of a work slowdown followed by a short strike. Mail service was severely disrupted. At one point, the General Post Office was forced to embargo all incoming foreign mail and it refused to accept any domestic mail for delivery. Some large British firms reserved seats on daily flights to Brussels or Paris and sent couriers to deposit outgoing foreign mail and pick up any incoming mail which the firms had been able to divert to these cities. But this expensive alternative was available to only a few. Most citizens and business firms had to exist without mail service.

A simple and straightforward way to reduce the threat of crippling strikes presented by the postal monopoly is to repeal the Private Express Statutes. Repeal would lead to development of viable alternatives which, in the event of a Postal Service strike, would provide limited but extremely useful capacity. Without making any presumptions about demands by workers or counterdemands by management, the existence of viable economic alternatives would clearly be an advantage to the public. Somewhat paradoxically, a good illustration of the advantages of having alternative delivery systems is provided by the United Parcel Service, which on more than one occasion has sustained a major strike that inconvenienced thousands of business firms and their customers. Fortunately, because of the widespread existence of alternatives (one of which was the Post Office), these tie-ups were "inconveniences" rather than total stoppages of commerce.

Will a prolonged postal strike be required before Congress and the body politic clearly perceive the need for repeal of the Private Express Statutes? We may speculate on a likely scenario which could lead to congressional action.

It will be recalled from Chapter III that the Postal Service is currently in the process of raising rates on most second- and third-class material to levels that will cover all attributable costs plus some reasonable share of the overhead. This will cause postage rates on these items to increase faster than labor costs in general, and these higher rates will almost surely result in the further development of private firms specializing in delivery of advertising materials and magazines. This trend is already under way and will continue if postal rates continue to increase according to plan. If the Private Express Statutes are not repealed, it is possible that within a few years a strike against the Postal Service will tie up all important letter mail—including social security checks, dividend checks, private correspondence, purchase orders, invoices and so on—while direct advertising matter ("junk" mail) and magazines (*Playboy, Penthouse, Hot Rod,* and so on) will be delivered regularly and promptly by private posts.

This situation, should it arise, would be likely to stimulate action—particularly if the postal strike were an extended one.

The social costs of a postal strike under existing monopoly conditions would be substantial. Since the public interest is never harmed by the creation of viable economic alternatives, public policy should not tolerate monopolies, public or private, unless there are overwhelming reasons for doing so—as with national security. No one, not even the Postal Service, can claim that a monopoly over letter mail is vital to our national security.

Incentives: Political versus Economic Decisions. When the Post Office was a regular governmental agency and its entire budget was subject to the congressional appropriations process, all capital expenditure decisions, including those for new postal facilities, were open to political influence. Congressmen traditionally tried to influence these decisions and obtain improved postal facilities for their districts. Rightly or wrongly, much of the blame for slow and inept decision making was attributed to Congress and the political process.

Congress finally responded to this situation by transferring authority for virtually all such decisions to the new Postal Service. One major consideration was the desire to insulate operating decisions from direct congressional supervision. In theory, the Postal Service is now supposed to be run as an efficient business enterprise, with management decisions no more vulnerable to political considerations than are the decisions of grocery chains or other private businesses. Unfortunately, the analogy to private enterprise is inexact if the enterprise in question is not subject to the discipline of the marketplace. Grocery store managers have incentives and are subject to controls by outside forces which simply do not exist for the postal monopoly.

One little-noted virtue of the former congressional budget review and appropriations process was that it contained a well-understood set of controls. Review by the Office of Management and Budget (formerly the Bureau of the Budget) and by Congress may not have been the best control process in the world but, in its own way, it put some useful constraints on postal managers. Doubtless better control systems exist. But did Congress in fact provide a better control system when it created the present Postal Service?

It is not clear what system of controls or incentives was established to replace those which previously existed. Congress created the Postal Rate Commission to inquire into and regulate postal rates. On questions concerning speed, regularity or dependability of mail service, the Postal Rate Commission has certain authority to investigate complaints—provided they are serious and widespread. On matters of facilities, mechanization, efficiency, and managerial incentives, it is unclear whether any outside authority or force now exerts control over the decisions of our professional postal managers. Even in the rate-making area, control is at best weak. So long as the Postal Service has a legal monopoly and is able to state what its costs are, it can in effect force the Postal Rate Commission to allow it to charge whatever the traffic will bear.

A well-known commentary on Boston runs as follows:

> And this is the city of Boston
> The home of the bean and the cod,
> Where Lowells speak only to Cabots,
> And Cabots speak only to God.

For the most part it appears that our professional postal managers have joined ranks with the Cabots and are now in a position where they too need answer only to God.[12] If ever a situation needed policing by Adam Smith's "invisible hand" of competition, it is this one.

It is unclear, moreover, whether Congress has effectively removed the undesirable aspects of political influence from management decisions. Of late, for example, civil rights groups have complained that the Postal Service is building many of its major new facilities in the suburbs, far from downtown areas. It is alleged that these suburban locations will make postal jobs less readily accessible to minority-group workers who live in central cities. As long as the Postal Service remains a government-sponsored monopoly, it is realistic to expect that all such decisions will continue to be the subject of political debate and lobbying efforts.

Future mechanization seems likely to offer similar problems. The Post Office has always been a labor-intensive operation but now some change may be in the wind. Over the past two decades the Post Office spent a relatively small but increasing amount of money on research and development aimed at the mechanization of mail sorting and processing. Despite the extensive public relations fanfare heralding a few experimental facilities, most mail is still sorted and processed by traditional means, but it may be hoped that the day is approaching when the Postal Service will be able to introduce widespread automation. However, the monopoly status of the Postal Service will make moves in this direction more political and thereby more difficult than they would be if the Postal Service were substantially open to competition from the private sector.

Undoubtedly the most constructive step which Congress could take to eliminate politics and impose economic rationality on the postal system would be to abolish the monopoly enshrined in the

Private Express Statutes. Since the Postal Service shows so little evidence of being a natural monopoly,[13] it is reasonable to expect that competition and market forces would provide postal management with strong positive incentives. At the same time competition would also be an effective regulator of potential abuses.

CHAPTER V

CONCLUSION

The Private Express Statutes had their beginnings in the royal carriage of the mails at least as far back as the sixteenth century. Whether the mail was a royal monopoly because only the kings had letters to send, or whether it was a royal monopoly because the kings were afraid of what their subjects would write, does not matter now. Neither case would give historical justification for the present postal monopoly.

Not that the U.S. postal monopoly is unconstitutional. It is clearly permitted by the Constitution and was indeed a natural thing in 1789 (or 1792). But what was natural then is not necessarily natural now.

The argument generally given for preserving the monopoly is that it protects postal revenues. This is an argument which in fact grants the truth of virtually every attack made on the Post Office or the Postal Service. The argument that postal revenues must be protected by a statutory monopoly has as its minor premise the belief that the Postal Service is so inefficient that it cannot stand up to competition—a premise which historical evidence suggests is true but which would seem to be damaging to the Postal Service.

Practically all major innovations in mail delivery seem to have come from private competitors rather than from the government monopoly—from Dockwra's penny post and Povey's bell-ringers, through the Pony Express (and other private express carriers at that time), down to the United Parcel Service of today. The areas in which the Postal Service seems best able to stand up to competition are those in which losses from present lower-than-market prices are subsidized by protected higher-than-market prices elsewhere. Of course, it is these higher-than-market prices which make the Postal Service vulnerable to competition, and which could make it even more vulnerable if the statutory protection were removed.

As Alfred Marshall pointed out long ago, arguments for the necessity of preserving postal revenues are specious. In 1974 the federal government can expect to collect in excess of $270 billion from all sources. In view of the government's ability to raise revenues of this magnitude, it should not be necessary to impose an admittedly inefficient postal monopoly on the public for the purpose of raising revenue. If the Postal Service, with its tax advantages, years of accumulated experience, and elements of natural monopoly (though they are not so great as claimed), cannot compete effectively, then private posts should be allowed to supplement government posts and deliver letter mail.

In fact, the cost of mail delivery under the protected monopoly is so high that some electric utility companies now use their own employees to deliver bills, private postal companies (of which the Independent Postal Service of America is the largest) now have delivery capacity to more than 10 million American homes, and the United Parcel Service prospers. But all of these represent only limited attacks on the postal behemoth. There would be substantial benefits from the open competition which would follow full repeal of the Private Express Statutes.

Overnight the Postal Service would have a remarkably increased incentive to improve efficiency and reduce costs. At the same time Congress would be assured that it could compare Postal Service costs, rates, and services to those of private competitors in order to determine whether operations were being kept under reasonable control, whether management was functioning well, or whether rates and costs were too high. Moreover, with private alternatives to the Post Office, short-run damage from postal strikes would be minimized.

If today's postal system is indeed subject to diseconomies of scale, as some research suggests, this constitutes an additional reason for repeal of the Private Express Statutes. Sound public policy would dictate that alternative private express companies be created as soon as possible. Substantial mail volume would be diverted to these companies, and the Postal Service could return to the range of efficient operation, thereby lowering its unit costs.

It is argued by the advocates of postal monopoly that private express companies would skim off the cream, leaving the Postal Service with only the unprofitable mail. But some of this unprofitable mail is supported by public service subsidies appropriated annually by Congress and so needs no "cream" for its support. Other mail (for example, rural deliveries) constitutes a natural monopoly and would not be skimmed off. Still other mail (for example, second-class deliveries) is unprofitable because rates are kept artificially low as a form of subsidy. As this subsidy is reduced, it is quite possible that private competitors will undercut the Postal Service here. If they do, then both the Postal Service and the users of first-class mails will be better off: the Postal Service will lose a "loss-leader" and first-class mail should receive better service.

If "cream-skimming" were allowed, doubtless the Postal Service would have to charge higher rates on high-cost and low-revenue mail not subject to public service subsidies, but the Postal Service, the cream-skimmers, and all other users of first-class mails would be better off.

The argument for continuing the monopoly—apart from the specious revenue argument—would be that certain users of first-class mails should be taxed to support other high-cost or low-revenue mail service. No evidence has been presented by the Postal Service or by any proponent of monopoly to show that this is socially or economically desirable. In fact, if it is believed that buyers should get what they pay for—not more and not less—then the present system is clearly inequitable, even iniquitous.

It may be pointed out that the channels of commerce have unquestionably been silted up by the postal monopoly. Enforcement of the Private Express Statutes has substantially impeded the development of better delivery services. In virtually every instance where private delivery services were forced out of business because of the postal monopoly, their principal "crime" was that of offering service to the public that the government mails would not offer.

In summary, Congress erred in not repealing the Private Express Statutes when it transformed the Post Office Department into the Postal Service. Neither the long history of postal monopoly nor concern for the current beneficiaries of its implicit taxation should stay Congress from setting the situation right. Mail communications are too important to be left to the mercy of a large and unresponsive monopolist.

EMPIRICAL EVIDENCE ON ECONOMIES OF SCALE

The purpose of this appendix is to provide a brief review of the various studies on economies of scale in the postal system. Readers wishing to pursue this subject further may refer to the sources cited here.

Two kinds of data are available for empirical studies of economies of scale, time series or cross-section data, and the following sections discuss both. In addition, a few productivity studies of the Post Office are available and are of some interest. These are discussed separately.

The subject of economies of scale arises frequently in discussions of postal policy. Yet worthwhile evidence on this subject is sparse. In general, postal authorities seem to accept the existence of economies of scale as an article of faith. For example, the President's Commission on Postal Organization and its contractor (Foster Associates, Inc.) accepted as "apparent" the waste that would result from competition.[1] The Board of Governors' recent submission to the President and Congress reaffirmed the faith.[2] It should be noted, though, that the Post Office is not known to have commissioned or undertaken any studies of its own on this subject, nor do the postal authorities cite any evidence to support their assertions and policy conclusions. Whether economies of scale do in fact exist is an open question.

When making management decisions related to economies of scale, postal authorities exhibit the courage of their convictions. They are at least consistent, even if consistently wrong. For example, as will be seen in the discussion of cross-section data, most evidence indicates that the largest facilities (with employment in the range 10,000 to 40,000 workers) have higher unit costs than smaller (medium-sized) facilities. Why this is so is not known, but the available evidence has not visibly influenced the design and construction of major postal facilities, where the benefit of size is accepted as an article of faith.

Time Series Data

Time series data confront an investigator with a number of well-known problems.[3] These problems are as applicable to the Postal Service as they are to any other industry. For example, mail is not a homogeneous commodity. It consists of letters, magazines, newspapers, parcels, and so on, and over time the mix has changed by significant amounts. The number of parcels has scarcely grown at all, but letter mail has generally shown year-to-year increases of between 3 and 5 percent. Thus the relative shares of parcel post and letter mail have changed. Yet because the concept of economies of scale is static, the mix is assumed to be constant over varying ranges of output. Time series data thus need to be adjusted for nonhomogeneity.

To complicate matters further for a study of economies of scale, letter mail itself has not been a homogeneous commodity over time. With the advent of electronic computers many companies have voluntarily presorted large mailings for the Postal Service, with the result that a substantial volume of letter mail now arrives at the local post office already sorted. Having all this sorting done for it is clearly an economy for the Postal Service, but at the same time it is by no means a scale economy of the postal system. If time series data are to be used, allowance must be made for this and other factors which have changed over the years.

Delivery presents another measurement problem. Economies of scale concern the behavior of unit costs for larger or smaller volumes of mail for a given technology. In other words, measurement of economies of scale attempts to ascertain whether a given delivery system, incorporating the best technology available at some given time, can handle increasing volume with decreasing costs. But time series data typically require observations over extended periods (ten years or more), and over such extended periods the route structure has always shown considerable change. New suburban routes have typically been more amenable to motorized delivery than routes in the older suburbs. Delivering an expanded volume of mail over an expanded route system is not the same thing as delivering more mail over a static route system. This requires still another adjustment in time series data.

Over time, the volume of mail has grown substantially, and part of this growth has been in volume per capita—the number of items mailed per year to each individual. Thus "scale" has increased, and if economies of scale do exist, they are presumably embedded in the total cost of the Postal Service. In order to isolate the effects of increased size, one must sort out at least three important factors from total cost data: (1) economies resulting from increased volume per capita or increased scale, (2) economies arising outside the Postal Service from factors such as increased computerization and presorting by large volume mailers (savings from sources outside the Post Office are not attributable to the size of the postal system), and (3) shifts in the cost curve which reflect changes in cost at all levels of operation, regardless of scale (this would include inflation, or savings related to mechanization where mechanization is not associated with the current scale of operations). Adjusting annual cost data to reflect these various changes while isolating unit cost changes attributable to increased scale is indeed a formidable task.

Because of these difficulties only one investigator, Stevenson, has attempted a full investigation of postal time series data. His recent study, based on time series data for the total postal system, found that

> the hypothesis of economies of scale could not be accepted, and . . . the hypothesis that diseconomies of scale exist tends to be borne out by the separate analysis of production functions, cost functions, and input factor demand functions, as well as by consideration of Kendrick type productivity measures. . . . What the present study does demonstrate is that the available data do not support the hypothesis that the Postal Service has been or is operating in a region where economies of scale are realized.[4]

Stevenson goes on to conclude:

> The findings . . . raise the question of the appropriateness of the Private Express Statutes. . . . Absent economies of scale, [the] rationale for protecting the Service from competition is without substantial merit. Indeed, the impact of the Private Express Statutes is to enable the Service to implement pricing and processing policies which are detrimental to the monopoly classes. The Private Express Statutes enable the Service to compete unfairly in those markets where it does not have legal protection by cross subsidizing the operations of the competitive services with excess revenues from the monopoly service. Such legal protection has had not only a detrimental effect upon the monopoly service, but also a chilling effect upon competition. The forestalling of competition could well result in a deterioration of service standards, sluggish technological

advancement and innovation, an increase in processing in-efficiencies, and a host of other performance problems. Thus it would be desirable to lift the legal prohibition against competition in the letter mail market, as well as the other restraints to competition with the USPS. This is not to say that the government should not be in the business of delivering mail. Rather, the government should not be pro-tected from competition from others who could provide similar services.[5]

One other author, Baratz, has examined time series data briefly, along with some cross-section data.[6] For the period studied, Baratz found slight increasing returns to scale.

Cross-section Data

The Postal Service has more than 20,000 separate post offices throughout the country. Many of these are small, but the postal organization might nevertheless appear to be a good subject for a cross-sectional study of economies of scale. However, just as there are knotty problems in dealing with time series data, so there are knotty problems in dealing with cross-section data.

One familiar problem is the nonhomogeneity of output. The output of an individual postal facility is the amount of processing performed on the mail which it handles. It happens that the amount of processing done in various facilities may differ substantially. For example, smaller and medium-sized post offices have recently been sending their mail to larger facilities for processing. Thus, the output of smaller post offices is not strictly comparable to that of larger post offices.

Among larger facilities the amount of processing may differ from time to time. To illustrate, the New York City post office will ordi-narily route all mail destined for northern California to San Francisco. After arrival in San Francisco, the mail will be sorted according to the exact city to which it is addressed—Oakland, Berkeley, Palo Alto, San Jose, and so on. However, if the San Francisco post office were to find itself in a temporary "crunch," then the New York City post office might do an extra sort on northern California mail to help relieve the San Francisco post office. When such instances occur the output of these two post offices would need to be adjusted to reflect these temporary changes.

The problem of adjusting for differential output is aggravated by the Postal Service's record-keeping system, which often does not record data significant for an empirical investigation of economies of scale.

Because of these problems, and possibly for other reasons as well, few investigators have attempted to compare costs and outputs of different sized post offices. The principal study is by Leonard Merewitz.[7]

Merewitz studied the cost-output relationship of the 156 largest post offices. These 156 offices were divided into three categories: small (approximately 250 to 500 employees), medium (600 to 1,500 employees), and large (2,000 to 40,000 employees). Merewitz concluded that the average cost curve for processing mail is distinctly U-shaped. That is, processing costs fall from the small to the medium range, then increase sharply for larger offices. According to Merewitz, "It is still an open question why productivity is low in the large offices." [8]

Processing costs are of course only part of the total picture. Merewitz also analyzed costs of other postal functions (acceptance, delivery, transportation, and administration). For the postal system as a whole he concluded that "in 1966 there appear to be economies of scale . . . up to offices of the size 1,400 employees. After that there appeared to be constant returns to scale." [9]

On the basis of these observed results, Merewitz drew a mixed set of policy conclusions. On the one hand he concluded that "there is not a good case for a monopoly on parcels." [10] On third-class mail he found, "That there is significant competition in third-class services suggests that postal rates are above average costs of these services. They should not be a protected monopoly because apparently other firms can produce them as cheaply as USPS." [11] At the same time, and in contrast to his preference for competition in third- and fourth-class mail, Merewitz recommended that "the monopoly on first-class mail should be retained and more vigorously enforced." [12] Merewitz acknowledged that subjecting the Postal Service to extensive competition might result in substantial lowering of cost regardless of scale of operation, but this did not cause him to change his conclusion on the postal monopoly.

Baratz [13] and Haldi [14] have also examined cross-section data, but in a more cursory fashion than Merewitz. Baratz concluded that the Post Office is probably subject to economies of scale and recommended retention of the postal monopoly. Haldi, on the other hand, concluded that economies of scale were not significant and recommended that the Private Express Statutes be repealed.

Productivity Data

The federal government in general and the Office of Management and Budget in particular have been far more interested in measuring increases in productivity from whatever source (including economies of scale) than in isolating and measuring economies of scale per se. Because of this interest in productivity measurement, there are studies on this subject, including studies of the Post Office.[15]

In view of the fact that other available data and evidence on economies of scale are so sparse, one should be aware of the productivity studies which have been done. At the same time, caution must be suggested in the interpretation of these studies. Data and conclusions from productivity studies are *at best* circumstantial evidence regarding economies of scale, and one must be extremely careful in drawing inferences from them. The best use of the studies of productivity may be as backup evidence to see whether they corroborate or negate conclusions from those studies whose purpose is to isolate economies of scale. That is, if large increases in productivity have been observed over periods when mail volume increased substantially, it would be incorrect to infer directly that economies of scale predominate in the postal system. By the same token, if mail volume increases substantially and no increase in productivity is observed, it would be equally incorrect to infer directly that the postal system is not subject to further economies of scale. Offsetting factors may have been at work in both cases.

Most attempts to measure postal productivity have found that productivity (volume of mail processed per worker) has scarcely changed over substantial periods of time although mail volume itself has increased substantially. This proves nothing but it is thoroughly consistent with either of the two following conclusions: (1) the postal system is subject to constant returns to scale, or (2) in its present size range, the postal system is subject to decreasing returns to scale but over time has managed to offset this negative factor by improved technology and mechanization. The observed constant productivity over time does put a heavy burden of proof on those who allege that the postal system is subject to extensive economies of scale. Although the evidence is circumstantial, results of past productivity studies would appear to support Stevenson more than Merewitz.

NOTES

NOTES TO INTRODUCTION

[1] The terms "Post Office" and "Postal Service" are used more or less interchangeably throughout this study. In general when the discussion is historical in nature an attempt has been made to use the term "Post Office," while "Postal Service" is reserved for discussion of current or future activities.

[2] 39 U.S.C. 601-606, and 18 U.S.C. 1693-1699, 1724.

[3] Joseph F. Johnston, Jr., "The United States Postal Monopoly," *The Business Lawyer,* vol. 23, no. 2 (January 1968), pp. 389-97.

NOTES TO CHAPTER I

[1] See Edward Gibbon, *The Decline and Fall of the Roman Empire* (New York: Modern Library, n.d.), vol. 1, p. 46.

[2] Howard Robinson, *The British Post Office, A History* (Princeton: Princeton University Press, 1948), p. 4.

[3] Ibid., p. 7.

[4] Ibid., p. 26.

[5] Ibid., p. 46.

[6] Ibid., pp. 67-68.

[7] Ibid., pp. 69-102.

[8] The Neale patent was later repurchased by the crown.

[9] See Harry Myron Konwiser, *Colonial and Revolutionary Posts* (Richmond: Dietz Press, 1931), pp. 16-17.

[10] Wesley Everett Rich, *The History of the United States Post Office to the Year 1829* (Cambridge: Harvard University Press, 1924), pp. 14-15.

[11] Konwiser, *Colonial and Revolutionary Posts,* p. 21.

[12] Rich, *History of U.S. Post Office,* pp. 43-44.

[13] Ibid., pp. 54-55.

[14] Ibid., pp. 56-57.

[15] Ex parte Jackson, 96 U.S. 727, 735 (1877) (dictum); United States v. Hall, 26 F. Cas. 75 (C.C. Pa. 1844); United States v. Thompson, 28 F. Cas. 97 (D. Mass. 1846); Williams v. Wells Fargo & Co. Express, 177 F. 352 (8th Cir. 1910). But, see *The Post-Office Monopoly,* 11 Monthly L. Rep. 385 (1849), for an argument that the monopoly is unconstitutional.

[16] See Lindsay Rogers, *The Postal Power of Congress: A Study in Constitutional Expansion* (Baltimore: Johns Hopkins University Studies in Historical and Political Science, 1916), p. 24.

[17] 1 Stat. 70.

[18] 1 Stat. 236.

[19] Various sections of the Private Express Statutes continue to apply to vessels today. See 18 U.S.C. 1695, 1698 and 1699. These provisions will not be considered in this study.

[20] 1 Stat. 360.

[21] 2 Stat. 592, section 16.

[22] 4 Stat. 102.

[23] 4 Stat. 238, section 3.

[24] The rate was 6 cents to 25 cents for a single sheet letter, depending on the distance. For two pieces of paper the rates were double; for three sheets, triple; and for four or more, quadruple.

[25] 24 F. Cas. 761 (S.D.N.Y. 1843). See also, United States v. Pomeroy, 27 F. Cas. 588 (N.D.N.Y. 1844).

[26] It must be remembered that at this time there was no law punishing the *sender.*

[27] 26 F. Cas. 782 (N.D.N.Y. 1844).

[28] Doc. No. 1, 28th Congress, 1st session, 596 et seq. (December 2, 1843) (United States Serial Set. No. 431, microfilm, New York Public Library).

[29] Ibid., p. 598. In other words, private carriers would skim off the cream from the low-cost, high-volume routes, leaving the Post Office Department with the less productive routes. The same argument was made later in the century by officials of the British Post Office Department, which was facing vigorous (and allegedly unlawful) competition from private posts. This argument was criticized by the economist Alfred Marshall, who contended that "if the State, with its enormous advantages for this particular business, can be undersold by private competitors, the reason must be either that it is extending its claim to the possession of business in regions where its special advantages fail, and where, therefore, there is no good reason for having the work done by a Government department with or without a monopoly, or else that it shows a grievous want of enterprise. It is idle to lay stress on the need of keeping up the Post Office revenue. For that part of the revenue which is reaped by the State as a result of its possessing the economies of production on a large scale would not be appreciably affected by the loss of its monopoly; and this is the only part of the revenue which is capable of being defended for a moment on economic grounds." Quoted in Ronald Coase, "The British Post Office and the Messenger Companies," *Journal of Law and Economics,* vol. 4, no. 1 (1961), pp. 12-50. Marshall is obviously arguing for a system of competitive pricing in the carriage of mail.

[30] 5 Stat. 732, sections 9-12.

[31] Act of August 31, 1852, section 8, 10 Stat. 121.

[32] Doc. No. 1, 29th Congress, 1st session, 845 et seq. (December 1, 1845) (United States Serial Set. No. 470). In the same report, the postmaster general anxiously noted the growing use of the telegraph and its potential adverse impact on the postal revenues and questioned whether "an instrument so powerful for good or for evil" should be left in private hands.

[33] Joshua Leavitt, *Cheap Postage* (Boston: Cheap Postage Association, 1848), p. 20.

[34] Ibid., p. 13.

[35] See *Postal Reform: Proceedings of a Public Meeting Held in the City of New York* (New York: Postal Reform Committee, 1856), p. 6, in which the chairman of the New York Postal Reform Committee stated that "the almost unanimous voice of public opinion declares that our Post Office is entirely inadequate to meet the wants of the people."

[36] 17 Stat. 283.

[37] 35 Stat. 1124.

[38] See 21 Op. Att'y Gen. 394, 398 (1896). The present applicable version of this exception is found in 18 U.S.C. 1694.

[39] 48 Stat. 1207.

[40] 62 Stat. 776.

[41] See 1 Stat. 232 (1792).

[42] 2 Stat. 592.

[43] 5 Stat. 736.

[44] 5 Stat. 735, section 9.

[45] Held lawful in United States v. Kochersperger, 26 F. Cas. 803 (C.C.E.D. Pa. 1860).

[46] 12 Stat. 204, section 4 (March 2, 1861).

[47] 17 Stat. 311, section 228 (June 8, 1872). See 39 U.S.C. 6105, declaring post roads to include "letter-carrier routes." The counterpart of this principle is that the streets of a town where U.S. mail delivery is not established are not post routes, and private persons may carry the mail within such a town. 3 Op. Asst. Att'y Gen. P.O.D. 162 (1897).

[48] Blackham v. Gresham, 16 F. 609 (C.C.N.Y. 1883).

[49] 3 Op. Asst. Att'y Gen. P.O.D. 137 (1895).

[50] 6 Op. Sol. P.O.D. 373 (1916).

[51] 2 Op. Sol. P.O.D. 482 (1887).

[52] 18 U.S.C. 1694, 1696.

[53] See United States Post Office Department, "Restrictions on Transportation of Letters," 5th ed., P.O.D. publication no. 111 (Washington: U.S. Government Printing Office, July 1967), p. 15.

[54] 4 Stat. 102, section 18.

[55] 5 Stat. 735.

[56] 18 F. 590 (S.D.N.Y. 1883).

[57] Ibid., p. 592.

[58] 6 Op. Sol. P.O.D. 403 (1916).

[59] U.S. Congress, House, *Hearings on H.R. 8869 before the Subcommittee of the House Committee on Post Office and Post Roads,* 74th Congress, 1st session (1935).

[60] The latter two exemptions will be discussed below.

[61] 18 U.S.C. 1694.

[62] Former 39 C.F.R., section 42.3(c), now omitted from the codified regulations. The former regulations as to who may carry letters have been retained as "uncodified regulations." See footnote 93, below.

[63] United States v. United States Express Co., 28 F. Cas. 352 (C.C. Ill. 1869). See 8 Op. Sol. P.O.D. 188, 189 (1932) (second opinion): "The Department cannot accept the view that the failure of the Congress to use the word 'exclusively' after 'relate' opens the door to all sorts of messages and communications however remotely they may relate to some article of cargo carried at the same time." In this opinion the department held that a bank statement accompanying canceled checks related not only to the checks but also contained live information with respect to the depositor's account, and accordingly did not come within the exemption.

[64] 18 U.S.C. 1694. See Post Office Department, "Restrictions on Transportation of Letters," pp. 16-18.

[65] 35 Stat. 1124.

[66] 21 Op. Att'y Gen. 394, 398 (1896); 1 Op. Asst. Att'y Gen. P.O.D. 910 (1884). However, in 1907 the department apparently shifted position in ruling that the Carnegie Steel Company could not lawfully use its own employees for providing messenger service between its own offices. 4 Op. Asst. Att'y Gen. P.O.D. 604. This may have prompted Congress to make the current business exemption explicit by putting it into the statute. See the discussion of the legislative history of the 1909 law in 28 Op. Att'y Gen. 537 (1910).

[67] "In general, if the person is an employee, he will share in all of the privileges enjoyed by other regular employees such as annual leave privileges and workmen's compensation insurance." See Post Office Department, "Restrictions on Transportation of Letters," p. 17.

[68] 18 U.S.C. 1696(a).

[69] 20 Stat. 356.

[70] 1 Op. Asst. Att'y Gen. P.O.D. 335 (1878).

[71] Post Office Department, "Restrictions on Transportation of Letters," p. 21.

[72] This was the position taken formerly in 39 C.F.R., section 42.3(f)(4), although it is not repeated in the current version of the codified regulations.

[73] 18 U.S.C. 1696(c).

[74] 5 Stat. 736.

[75] United States v. Thompson, 28 F. Cas. 97 (D. Mass. 1846).

[76] 8 Op. Sol. P.O.D. 201 (1932).

[77] 18 U.S.C. 1696(c).

[78] 1 Stat. 236.

[79] See text at note 54.

[80] 8 Op. Sol. P.O.D. 185, 186 (1932).

[81] 39 U.S.C. 601, providing as follows:

"(a) A letter may be carried out of the mails when—

"(1) it is enclosed in an envelope;

"(2) the amount of postage which would have been charged on the letter if it had been sent by mail is paid by stamps, or postage meter stamps, on the envelope;

"(3) the envelope is properly addressed;

"(4) the envelope is so sealed that the letter cannot be taken from it without defacing the envelope;

"(5) any stamps on the envelope are canceled in ink by the sender; and

"(6) the date of the letter, of its transmission or receipt by the carrier is endorsed on the envelope in ink."

"(b) The Postmaster General may suspend the operation of any part of this section upon any mail route where the public interest requires the suspension."

[82] 10 Stat. 121, section 8. See text at note 31 supra.

[83] *Towards Postal Excellence: The Report of the President's Commission on Postal Organization* (Washington, D. C.: U.S. Government Printing Office, 1968).

[84] Ibid., p. 129.

[85] Ibid.

[86] Ibid., p. 128.

[87] Ibid., p. 129.

[88] 39 U.S.C.A. 201.

[89] 39 U.S.C.A. 601, formerly 39 U.S.C.A. 901.

[90] National Association of Letter Carriers v. Independent Postal System of America, Inc., 336 F. Supp. 804 (W.D. Okla. 1971), *aff'd* 470 F. 2d 265 (10th Cir. 1972).

[91] National Association of Letter Carriers v. Independent Postal System of America, Inc., 336 F. Supp. at 806.

[92] 39 U.S.C.A. 601 and 18 U.S.C.A. 1696.

[93] The court noted that the current regulation, formerly 39 C.F.R., section 152.2, has been retained as an "uncodified regulation" in 35 Federal Register, section 19399 (1970). See 39 C.F.R., p. 7, and part 152.

[94] National Association of Letter Carriers v. Independent Postal System of America, Inc., 470 F.2d 265 (10th Cir. 1972).

[95] 470 F. 2d at 270.

[96] American Postal Workers Union v. Independent Postal System of America, Inc., 349 F. Supp. 1297 (E.D. Mich. 1972). This case was recently affirmed by the Sixth Circuit Court of Appeals, 42 Law Week 2058, June 26, 1973. The court held that the labor union lacked standing to sue and specifically rejected the contrary conclusion of the Tenth Circuit. The United States Supreme Court has agreed to review this decision; see 42 Law Week 3358 (December 18, 1973).

[97] See 38 Federal Register 17512-17516 (July 2, 1973). Also see *The Private Express Statutes and Their Administration,* A Report by the Board of Governors to the President and the Congress, pursuant to Section 7 of the Postal Reorganization Act, United States Postal Service (Washington: U.S. Government Printing Office, June 29, 1973).

[98] 38 Federal Register 17512.

[99] 38 Federal Register 17513.

[100] 38 Federal Register 17515.

[101] Ibid.

[102] Ibid.

NOTES TO CHAPTER II

[1] Carl Scheele, *A Short History of the Mail Service* (Washington, D. C.: Smithsonian Institution Press, 1970), p. 83.

[2] *Encyclopedia Britannica,* 1971 edition, vol. 18, p. 312.

[3] *Wall Street Journal,* December 20, 1972, p. 1.

[4] Congress has established the size limits on parcels which can be accepted by the Post Office. If these limits are unduly restrictive, it is in no small part due to the successful lobbying efforts of the Railroad Express Agency (now REA), which has a long record of opposing the competition which larger size limits would engender. The UPS limits are ICC-regulated and approved, but they reflect limits requested by UPS.

[5] *Business Week,* July 18, 1970, p. 94.

[6] *U.S. News & World Report,* June 25, 1973, p. 43.

[7] *Wall Street Journal,* December 20, 1972, p. 21.

[8] *Business Week,* July 18, 1970, p. 96.

[9] *Wall Street Journal,* December 20, 1972, p. 1. (Emphasis added.)

[10] *New York Times,* October 11, 1973.

[11] *U.S. News & World Report,* November 1, 1971, pp. 24-25.

[12] Leonard Merewitz, "The New Public Utility: Postal Prospects," mimeographed paper delivered to Seminar on Problems of Regulation and Public Utilities, September 1, 1972, at Dartmouth College, Hanover, New Hampshire.

[13] *U.S. News & World Report,* November 1, 1971, p. 24.

[14] Interview with *U.S. News & World Report,* June 25, 1973.

[15] But see Chapter I, p. 16, for a discussion of litigation brought by a postal union against IPSA involving the delivery of Christmas cards.

[16] *U.S. News & World Report,* November 1, 1971, p. 25.

[17] *U.S. News & World Report,* June 25, 1973, p. 43.

[18] Private correspondence, June 7, 1973.

[19] First-class rates will increase from eight to ten cents per ounce, effective March 2, 1974, on an interim basis pending review by the Postal Rate Commission.

NOTES TO CHAPTER III

[1] Defining "attributable" cost and "fair share" presents a thorny problem to the Postal Rate Commission. This subject will be discussed later.

[2] In the first rate hearing before the newly created Postal Rate Commission, the Postal Service claimed that just a shade more than 50 percent of its total costs were "directly attributable" to the various classes of mail. That so few costs can be directly attributable seems rather extraordinary in view of the fact that capital costs are low and 80-85 percent of all costs are labor-related, with a substantial portion of the remainder going for purchased transportation (most of which costs are directly attributable). The chief examiner rightly admonished the Postal Service to do its homework better before subsequent proceedings.

[3] Technically, the law governing parcel post rates also appears to preclude the possibility of significant subsidy by requiring that parcel post rates be set between 96 and 104 percent of full cost. However, different interpretations of "full cost" would permit wide variations in rates and the costs which could be allocated to parcel post. The existence of viable independent competition has policed and restrained unjustified parcel post rates much better than any regulatory body—or laws and regulations governing full costs.

[4] Electronic data transmission has already eroded postal revenues. For example, postal regulations interpret the definition of a "letter" to include punched computer cards and such cards are therefore required to be shipped by first-class mail unless some specific exemption applies, such as a firm using its own employees to transport cards from one location to another. This attempt to restrict commerce or communications to postal channels loses impact each year as more and more data are transmitted electronically.

[5] For seven specific examples, see Board of Governors, *The Private Express Statutes and Their Administration,* Appendix E, "Competition of the Postal Service Related to the Private Express Statutes," pp. 11-12.

6 For example, in its review of the Private Express Statutes the President's Commission cn Postal Organization (the Kappel Commission) said, "The postal service is particularly vulnerable to 'cream-skimming' in high-volume, high-value segments of its market, e.g., delivery within or between downtown business districts of major cities." (*Towards Postal Excellence,* p. 129.) More recently, this position was reiterated: "We recommend that the restrictions on private carriage of letters be retained. . . . To do otherwise would permit cream-skimming competition in the most profitable postal markets. . . ." (Board of Governors, *The Private Express Statutes and Their Administration,* cover letter to the President.)

7 It seems unlikely that any firm subject to antitrust prosecution would ever raise charges of cream-skimming, since this complaint would constitute prima facie evidence of a noncompetitive market.

8 "Chances for Better Mail Service," interview with Postmaster General Elmer T. Klassen, *U.S. News & World Report,* June 25, 1973, p. 43.

9 It should be pointed out that the high-cost part of postal operations is the labor cost involved in sorting and processing mail. A letter from one relatively obscure place to another may have to be handled and rehandled—"massaged" in the vernacular of the Post Office—many times before final delivery. The direct cost of transportation is a relatively small part of the total cost and should play only a minor role in discussions of cream-skimming. First-class letters are transported by air (the most expensive means) at 0.3 cents out of 8 cents postage or 0.4 cents out of 11 cents air mail postage (see Air Transport Association of America, *Airline Newsletter,* Summer 1973). This amounts to 3.75 percent and 3.64 percent of total postage costs, respectively. The other 96-plus percent goes for operating costs of the Postal Service.

10 The Postal Service has conducted a study to determine what price level and profit level a competitor might be able to achieve for certain portions of first-class mail. According to this study, mailers could receive savings of 40 to 45 percent from present rates and, after paying state and local taxes from which the Postal Service is exempt, the new private firm would receive a 32 percent return on equity (on which federal income taxes would be payable). These figures are astounding. They indicate the extent to which some mailers are being subjected to monopolistic price gouging. Interestingly, the study assumes that the new private firm would pay the same rates and have the same cost structure as the Postal Service (i.e., cost rates equal to those found in the Post Office were assumed throughout). If the new firm achieved any efficiencies or cost savings, its return would be even greater.

11 Board of Governors, *The Private Express Statutes and Their Administration,* Appendix E, pp. 16-17. (Emphasis added.)

12 John Haldi, "The Value of Output of the Post Office Department," in J. Margolis, ed., *The Analysis of Public Output* (New York: National Bureau of Economic Research, 1970), pp. 339-80; see especially p. 365.

13 It was noted previously (note 29 in Chapter I) that Alfred Marshall long ago argued for replacing statutory monopoly with competitive pricing of postal services.

NOTES TO CHAPTER IV

1 Existing evidence on this subject is somewhat skimpy and collectively inconclusive. However, one of the most recent econometric studies on this subject indicates that our existing postal system may in fact be subject to extensive *diseconomies* of scale. See Rodney E. Stevenson, "Postal Pricing Problems and Production Functions" (Ph.D. dissertation, Michigan State University, Department of Economics, 1973).

2 Quoted in Ronald Coase, "The British Post Office and the Messenger Companies," *Journal of Law and Economics,* vol. 4, no. 1 (1961), pp. 12-50. Marshall is arguing for a system of competitive pricing in the carriage of mail.

³ Fortunately, these high-cost routes constitute a small and declining portion of the entire postal system. It would be wrong to infer that the system as a whole is a natural monopoly because one small component is.

⁴ If private competitors were allowed to exist and they somehow acquired mail (e.g., by mistake) for delivery in rural areas, it seems almost certain that they would simply deposit it in the U.S. mail for delivery.

⁵ It should be noted that the arguments employed by the postal authorities to defend the Private Express Statutes (see Board of Governors, *The Private Express Statutes and Their Administration*) could also be used to justify extension of the Private Express Statutes to all other classes of mail, including parcel post. Despite this fact, the postal authorities only defend the status quo and make no argument or request for extending their monopoly.

⁶ The excess capacity and high sunk cost embodied in the railroad network serving the northeastern United States is a real-life example of excessive zeal in building capital-intensive public utilities.

⁷ Board of Governors, *The Private Express Statutes and Their Administration*, p. 9.

⁸ In previous years the practice of levying charges only on the sender led to development of a "fully allocated" cost accounting system, which attempted to assign all costs of the postal system to different classes of mail. Under the rules of this cost ascertainment system, all costs were allocated, including route carriers' salaries and overhead items such as the postmaster general's salary, depreciation on buildings, and expenditures on research and development. This annual exercise in futility was carried out through a labyrinth of arbitrary rules which completely ignored the fact that many overhead items and many differential delivery costs are in no way attributable either to a single class of mail or even to all classes of mail combined.

⁹ It is quite possible that today's postal system is a victim of serious diseconomies of scale and rising unit costs. The cost of managing such a labor-intensive operation may in fact be rising disproportionately as the scale of operation increases. In this event repeal of the Private Express Statutes is long overdue and would constitute one of the kindest things that could be done to the Postal Service.

¹⁰ As noted, the Postal Service already receives a public service subsidy for all deficits incurred on RFD routes. There would be no need to raise rates or lower quality of service on these routes.

¹¹ This method of analysis is in keeping with the usual economic distinction between movements along a unit-cost curve and downward shifts in the cost curve.

¹² It is interesting to observe that although the President's announced public policy is to limit price increases in the private sector to 3 to 4 percent per year, the Postal Service has already announced its intention to request an increase in first-class postage rates of 25 percent effective in March 1974.

¹³ Volume 3 of the Annex to *Towards Postal Excellence: The Report of the President's Commission on Postal Organization*, p. 128, notes that "the recent attempts to establish private posts contravene a long tradition of postal monopoly *but the postal monopoly itself is a matter of legislative preferment for the protection of revenue rather than a natural monopoly.*" (Italics added.) See also Stevenson, "Postal Pricing Problems and Production Functions."

NOTES TO APPENDIX

¹ The Kappel Commission, *Towards Postal Excellence*, p. 128.

² Board of Governors, *The Private Express Statutes and Their Administration*, p. 9 and Appendix F, pp. 4-14.

³ See Haldi and Whitcomb, "Economies of Scale in Industrial Plants," *Journal of Political Economy*, vol. 75, no. 4, part 1 (1967), pp. 373-385; also Caleb

Smith, "A Survey of Empirical Evidence on Economies of Scale," *Business Concentration and Price Policy* (Princeton, N.J.: Princeton University Press, 1955), pp. 193-229.

[4] Stevenson, "Postal Pricing Problems and Production Functions," pp. 91-92.

[5] Ibid., pp. 95-96.

[6] Morton S. Baratz, *The Economics of the Postal Service* (Washington, D. C.: Public Affairs Press, 1962). See especially pp. 26-34.

[7] Leonard Merewitz, *The Production Function in the Public Sector: Production of Postal Services in the Post Office* (Monograph 14, Center for Planning and Development Research, University of California, Berkeley, 1969). Also by the same author: (1) "Costs and Returns to Scale in U.S. Post Offices," *Journal of the American Statistical Association,* September 1971 and (2) "The New Public Utility: Postal Prospects."

[8] Merewitz, "The New Public Utility: Postal Prospects," p. 26.

[9] Ibid.

[10] Ibid., p. 27. In buttressing this conclusion, Merewitz notes that parcels are delivered on separate routes. When discussing first-class mail he maintains that the delivery system is subject to substantial economies of scale and concludes that the monopoly on first-class mail should be retained. The almost contradictory reasoning and conclusions are not explained.

[11] Ibid. Thus for third-class mail Merewitz is willing to accept competition on the basis of the fact that postal rates are above costs. First-class rates are also above costs, but Merewitz implicitly rejects this same line of reasoning applied to first-class mail.

[12] Ibid.

[13] Morton S. Baratz, *The Economics of the Postal Service.*

[14] John Haldi, "The Value of Output of the Post Office Department," in J. Margolis, ed., *The Analysis of Public Output.*

[15] F. Dziadek, "The Productivity of the United States Post Office: An Intertemporal and Cross-Sectional Study of Post Office Labor Productivity" (Ph.D. dissertation, Johns Hopkins University, 1969); United States Post Office Department, *Measurement of Productivity of the Post Office Department* (Washington, D. C.: Bureau of Finance, December 1963); Nestor Terleckyj, "Recent Trends in Output and Input of the Federal Government" (Paper given at the annual meeting of the American Statistical Association, Chicago, Illinois, December 27, 1973); Executive Office of the President, Bureau of the Budget, "Measuring Productivity in the Federal Government" (Washington: U.S. Government Printing Office, 1964).

70

Book design: Pat Taylor